THE ISL
CIVILIZATION

DR. MUSTAFA SIBAʿĪ

TRANSLATION REVISED BY
S.M. HASAN AL-BANNA

AWAKENING

PUBLISHED BY THE PRESS SYNDICATE OF AWAKENING PUBLICATIONS
Uplands Business Centre, Bernard Street, Swansea, SA2 0DR, United Kingdom

AWAKENING PUBLICATIONS

Uplands Business Centre, Bernard Street, Swansea, SA2 0DR, United Kingdom

P.O. Box 360009, Milpitas, CA 95036, United States of America

First Published in July 2002/Rabīʿ al-Thānī 1423

Printed by R.R. Donnelley & Sons, USA

Typeset in Bembo 11/14 [CP]

A catalogue record for this book is available from the British Library

Library of Congress cataloging in publication data

THE ISLAMIC CIVILIZATION

by Dr. Mustafa Siba'i

translation revised by S.M. Hasan al-Banna

p. cm.

Includes bibliographical references

ISBN 0 9537582 6 5

1. Islam - General - History. 1. Title.

بسم الله الرحمن الرحيم

DR. MUSTAFA SIBAᶜĪ was born in 1915 in the city of Hams, Syria. He memorised the Quran at a very young age. He studied the Islamic Sciences with his father Shaykh Hasani Sibaᶜī and in circles with great scholars and jurists of Hams. From the young age of eighteen he used to deliver the Friday *khuṭbah*s in the absence of his father. In 1933, he went to Egypt and enrolled at the University of Al-Azhar to study *fiqh*. Upon completing his studies in fiqh, he enrolled at the *Uṣūl al-Dīn* Faculty of Al-Azhar and excelled in his studies. In 1949, he completed his Ph.D. on the theme of "The Position of *Sunnah* in Legislation." In 1950, he was appointed Professor of Law at the University of Damascus, and in 1955, he established the Faculty of Sharīᶜah at the same university. He established the Muslim Brotherhood in Syria in 1945. Dr. Sibaᶜī was elected to the Syrian Parliament from 1949-1954. He passed away in 1964.

CONTENTS

FOREWORD

"There once was a civilization that was the greatest in the world. It was able to create a continental super-state that stretched from ocean to ocean and from northern climes to tropics and deserts. Within its dominion lived hundreds of millions of people, of different creeds and ethnic origins.

One of its languages became the universal language of a large part of the world and the bridge between the peoples of a hundred lands. Its armies were made up of people of many nationalities, and its military protection allowed a degree of peace and prosperity that had never been known. The reach of this civilization's commerce extended from Latin America to China, and everywhere in between.

And this civilization was driven more than anything, by invention. Its architects designed buildings that defied gravity and its mathematicians created algebra and algorithms that would enable the building of computers and the creation of encryption. Its physicians examined the human body and found new cures for disease, whilst its astronomers looked into the heavens, named the stars, and paved the way for space travel and exploration. Its writers created thousands of stories—stories of courage, romance and magic. Its poets wrote of love, when others before them were too steeped in fear to think of such things.

When other nations were afraid of ideas, this civilization thrived on them and kept them alive. When the censors threatened to wipe out knowledge from past civilizations, this civilization kept the knowledge alive and passed it on to others.

While modern Western civilization shares many of these traits, the civilization I'm talking about was the Islamic world from the year 800 to 1600, which included the Ottoman Empire and the courts of Baghdad, Damascus and Cairo, and such enlightened rulers as Sulaymān the Magnificent.

Although we are often unaware of our indebtedness to this other civilization, its gifts are very much a part of our heritage. The technology industry would not exist without the contributions of Arab mathematicians. Sufi poet-philosophers like Rūmī challenged our notions of self and truth, and leaders like Sulaymān contributed to our notions of tolerance and civic leadership.

Perhaps we can learn a lesson from this example: It was leadership based on meritocracy, not inheritance. It was leadership that harnessed the full capabilities of a very diverse population, which included Christian, Islamic and Jewish traditions.

This kind of enlightened leadership that nurtured culture, sustainability, diversity and courage led to 800 years of invention and prosperity.

In these dark and serious times, we must affirm our commitment to building societies and institutions that aspire to this kind of greatness. More than ever, we must focus on the importance of leadership, both bold acts of leadership and decidedly personal acts of leadership."

The preceding descriptions are not the words of a famous Muslim scholar, but those of Carly Fiornia, the CEO of Hewlett Packard, ending her speech on "Technology, Business and Our Way of Life: What's Next?" held in Minnesota (September 2001).

Dr. Tara Chand, a distinguished scholar and historian of India, said, in his Presidential address to the "Fourth All India Islamic Studies Conference" in December 1964, "For a thousand years this civilization was the central light whose rays illumined the world. It was the mother of European culture, for men reared in this civilization were the masters in the Middle Ages at whose feet the Spaniards, the French, the English, the Italians and the Germans sat to learn philosophy, science, mathematics, astronomy, chemistry, physics, medicine and industrial techniques. Their names were household words."

One could quote more statements of historians, academics, leaders and thinkers who, despite not being Muslims themselves, highlight the contribution of Islam to human civilization. Is it such a surprise that those who do not adhere to the Islamic faith can hold the civilization it created in such high regard? I think not.

Islamic Civilization was a blessing for humanity at large and not just for those who believed in the Islamic faith. The examples of justice, intellectual advancement, philanthropy, vibrant culture, equality, tolerance and morality are yet to be paralleled by any other human civilization. It was because the Prophet Muḥammad ﷺ was sent as a mercy to mankind that the civilization he built could only have mercy and justice as its foundations.

The challenge facing the Muslims of today is the reconstruction of this great Islamic Civilization and the revival of its unique legacy. Revival is required in every strata of human society with comprehensive problems requiring comprehensive solutions. Two essential elements are required for such a program of revival: vision and power. In the words of the great poet and philosopher Muhammad Iqbal, "Vision without power does bring moral elevation but cannot give a lasting culture. Power without vision tends to become destructive and inhuman. Both must combine for the expansion of humanity."

This book written by Dr. Mustafa Sibaʿī (1915 – 1964) is a collection of lectures he delivered on Syrian Radio between September and December 1955. Dr. Mustafa Sibaʿī was a leading figure of the Muslim Brotherhood as well as being a great scholar of Islam. Shaykh Abul-Ḥasan ʿAlī Nadwī says about him, "He is an embodiment of steadfastness. His long struggle spread over different fields—from the battlefield of Palestine to the Syrian Parliament, from the office of the leader [of the Muslim Brotherhood in Syria] to the oceans of compiling, writing and journalism, from the pulpit of speech and *daʿwah* to the idea of establishing the Faculty of *Sharīʿah* at the Syrian University, from debating with atheist orientalists to guiding and directing the Muslim youth…a struggle which was never interrupted and continued to the very last day of his life."

The book was first translated into English by the International Islamic Federation of Student Organizations (IIFSO) in 1984, but the translation was incomplete and required revisions so as to bring it closer to the original Arabic. The current edition is thus largely a revised translation with extensive editing. For the sake of clarity many amendments were necessary. It should be noted when reading the book that listeners were originally intended as the audience and this is reflected in the style of writing.

Finally, I would like to thank Bara al-Ghannouchi, Tim Bowes, Muhsina Thaherah, Nadīm Hussain, Maqbul Ali, Atia Azmi, Wassim Malak, Razia Fatima, and Omar Williams for their invaluable help in the production of this book. Shaykh Abul-ᶜAynayn and Abd al-Kawy also facilitated the production of this book in numerous ways whilst I was in Alexandria completing the revised translation. May Allah reward them all with the best of rewards.

S. M. Hasan al-Banna
October 2001, London, UK

INTRODUCTION

ALL PRAISES ARE for Allah, Lord of the Worlds. May the peace and blessings of Allah be upon the founder of the noblest civilization known to history—our leader Prophet Muḥammad, upon his family and his Companions who built the structure of that civilization with their blood and efforts. They have the virtue of everyone who has been blessed by its goodness till the Day of Judgment.

The modern period has surpassed every other period in material progress and scientific discoveries. Despite this progress, the scholars of Sociology, Psychology and Medicine are amazed at the alarming increase in the number of neurotics and those suffering from other nervous disorders. An atmosphere of worry and fear pervades the whole world, particularly in the civilized countries, in which the future of humanity appears dark. People find themselves bereft of all pleasure, even in the super-abundance of social amenities and a life of ease and luxury. The utopia or, at least, the golden period that the learned men and thinkers of the nineteenth century had contemplated on the basis of the scientific inventions and discoveries soon became a confused dream.

It appears that the greater the progress of the means at man's disposal, the more his restlessness and anxiety becomes. The countries with a very high standard of living have a greater percentage of psychological illnesses than in other not-so-privileged countries. This is clearly indicated by the statistics published by the government of the United States. This worry is not due to two world wars or the fear of a third, but the outcome of the psychological atmosphere provided by the modern civilization for its inhabitants. Although the colonial powers are constantly creating conditions which keep the nations under their influence, the restlessness pervades even those nations that have apparently escaped becoming the target of imperialism. It has taken into its grip even those nations that have benefited immensely through the exploitations of the colonial powers. Such anxiety is found even in societies established on new social theories and principles. The same restlessness is realized in the entire East and West, and the uneasiness is even reflected in the [former] Socialist order of Soviet Russia.

The proof of this agitated state of mind is provided by the large number of suicides so common among the civilized and highly cultured nations of the world. The most amazing among these are the incidents occurring in the Scandinavian countries which are known as the highest developed countries in the world both economically and culturally. More amazing is the fact that some of the people of those countries commit suicide simply because they get 'sick' of their luxurious pattern of living. It seems that this anxiety, tension and moral deviation, which has raised a cry of protest from parents in the West itself, is a result of the modern Western civilization and of the philosophical principles which lay at its foundation.

The modern Western civilization came into existence from contact of the West with Islamic Civilization through the Arab centres established in Spain and other Muslim countries. The scholars and philosophers of the Islamic world were very much interested in Greek philosophy. So it was from these Arab philosophers that the intelligent students of the West picked up Greek philosophy, rendered their books into their own language, and notwithstanding the strong opposition of the Church, set out to study them and propagate their teachings. When the Western nation had acquired such broad vision, they inferred these facts which were diametrically opposed to the knowledge and teachings of the church and a long struggle ensued between the church and science. Having suffered an exasperating course of imprisonment, inquisitions, verdicts of heresy and excommunications, the philosophers and the thinkers were at long last victorious in their struggle. When this renaissance movement of the West could stand on its own two feet, it had the clear stamp of two things—love of Greek philosophy, formed with purely materialistic and idolatrous concepts, and disgust of religion and the animosity of the religious and their rebellion against them. Hence, we find that the opinions of the Western thinkers were formed and developed under these two factors. It is in the light of these powerful elements that all the philosophical and moral schools of the West have developed and these are the beliefs underlying the Western mind and heart to this day.

Thus, the basis of Western Civilization is materialistic and far removed from the spirituality of religion and its intrinsic effects. This has resulted in religion losing its influence and authority in the Western countries, and the man in the West finds himself drifting towards the deepest abyss of degradation, confronted with the severest anxiety and apprehension. The visionary Western thinkers and others who want to review and bring into action the spiritual values of religion have as yet been unable to do so. The cult of atheism and materialism is now deeply rooted in Western Civilization.

One of the characteristics of religion—divine religion—is that it develops justice and equality, satisfies the heart and the soul, reduces the pain of misery and trouble, and lightens the burden of life. In addition, it relieves man of carnal urges and ignoble passions. Islam, in its heyday, had accomplished this feat. However, when this pure and divine mission ceased to direct collective life and when the effective weapons awakening the aspirations in individuals and rousing their resolutions and passions of sacrifice and affection became blunt, we tasted the bitterness of misery.

It is not the aim here to judge the dispute between the Western Civilization and religion. Suffice it to point out the causes of the poverty of this civilization and culture due to which it has proved miserably inadequate and helpless in conferring tranquillity in the soul and mind of man. The reason lies in the fact that when this civilization parted from religion and carved out a path for itself, it deviated far from that religion and ever since it has been engaged in a life and death struggle against it.

It took the hypothetical stand that it could continue its journey, all alone, without having recourse to any other faith which may be helpful in keeping its soul fresh and its conscience alive. However, this was an erroneous notion and today we are once again witnessing the emergence of a sincere passion for mutual cooperation between the various governments of the Western countries and the religious institutions in order to lessen the bitterness and devastation of Western Civilization. Whenever I have been in the Western countries, I have observed that several methods and various means are being put into practice to achieve this end.

Anyone who has toured Switzerland recently must certainly have observed a procession accompanied by a musical band moving about parks and other places of recreation. These religious processions are arranged by the church, and are made up of both young and old, men and women, who grab the attention of people by chanting hymns and songs of praise to musical accompaniment. A crowd thus gathers round them and everyone is invited to listen to the speakers in the procession.

Anyone visiting London's Hyde Park can hear speeches being delivered that are open to all. Among the speakers, there are preachers of the church, whose endeavour is to grab the attention of the greater part of the crowd in the park through their eloquence and effective style of speaking. Similarly, in areas that are particularly frequented for their cinemas, one often witnesses, in a noisy crowd, a person ascending a stage, held in position by his companion. The person on the stage harangues people on the theme of religion. One night, I saw a person standing in the doorway of a cinema, loudly warning people against the evil effects of cinema on their morality. All this was going on in the presence of the police who did not in the least object to it or obstruct their path. Some people listened to him attentively but I did not see any person thinking for himself and abstain from entering the cinema.

It is common practice in Europe and America for a society or a recreation club where young boys and girls dance and sing and enjoy themselves chatting, joking and having fun to be associated with the Church and travel together and hold meetings in the church. I happened to attend such a meeting, and noticed that they had on their program singing, playing musical instruments, eating, drinking and staying awake during the nights and nothing else. I asked their manager, "Do you also present religious teachings and preaching to the participants in your meetings?" The answer was no. I asked him, "Why then does the church arrange and put up with all the expenses of these societies and their meetings when they are very much like other societies with which the church has nothing to do?" He said in reply, "Is it not enough that boys and girls come into the church to participate in the meetings of the society, and in this way they have the existence of the church also in their minds?"

Anyone who has travelled Europe cannot fail to notice in some hotels a copy of Bible on the bedside table supplied by the Association of the Lovers of the Holy Bible. The aim underlying this practice is obviously to induce the traveller to look through it before going to bed or when waking up in the morning, thus reviewing his faith and belief. In most universities of Europe there are organizations under the name of the Christian Students' Union whose weekly meetings are addressed by a minister of the church who presents the principles and basic tenets of the Christian religion, with some students also participating in the discussion.

The government of West Germany imposes and collects a national fund in the name of the Church so that it may help in the propagation of Christianity. I once saw in the hospital attached to the Cologne University in West Germany, a huge bronze cross placed on the wall of my ward in front of my bed. Later, I discovered that such crosses were placed in every room. I enquired about the wisdom underlying these fixtures, and was told that it was a tactic employed by the church to remind people of their religion. All this was there in spite of the fact that the hospital was run by the university and had no direct link with the church.

I can never forget the many religious films produced in Hollywood, which have held people spellbound. Many of us must have heard of the moral rearmament organizations which exist in most European countries. Their representatives have toured the Middle East and the Far East. These organizations apparently stress only moral excellence and mercy and justice.

This is a brief account of the activities that continue in the Western countries for the revival of religion and morality, and they very explicitly elucidate the point that the Western nations, in order to lessen the evils of their civilization and culture, have come to realize that they need to enlist the aid of religion and morals. However, in spite of all these efforts, such control is not in the hands of the religious leaders, moral teachers and social experts. They have had the opportunity; calamities and afflictions are now on the increase, and this civilization must come to realize this problem.

The fact remains that the desire to work towards a return to religion and towards the elevation of the spiritual level of the common people must also contend with the dread of the propagation and domination of Socialism. However, religion in Europe, due to its poor condition and the skeptical attitude created by the Western philosophies, is totally incapable of confronting Socialism. Therefore, social and economic measures have become the inevitable barricade against the onslaught of the Red Menace. Materialistic intellect such as the Western intellect cannot perceive anything other than the material. Neither can it agree to anything else. Socialism is a branch of the same evil tree and one of its bitter fruits.

The Socialist philosophy of Marx and Engels appeared on the political horizon in the nineteenth century. The conditions became all the worse because of this philosophy, since it created a wide gulf between man and his spiritual solace. Thus, the belief in God and the Hereafter departed from their hearts, and the moral foundations on which human societies have been based on since the dawn of time for collective peace and tranquillity collapsed. The first ever dominion claiming to uphold the principles of Communism had come into existence, and tried to improve the lot of its people. Yet it miserably failed in its attempt and could never succeed in its objective of removing every form of anxiety and restlessness from the individual and collective life of its people, and rid them of all apprehension and terror, due to its materialistic philosophy of life. Furthermore, the Communist State has clamped some additional dreads on its citizens, and maintains that anyone found to be criticizing the State and its policies must come to an unhappy end. Again, the mental perturbation and fear that haunts the members of the Communist parties is much greater than that pervading the minds of the common citizens of the Communist State. It forces every member of the Communist party to loudly support every suggestion, every opinion of their leaders and defend and follow them blindly or else be resigned to the fate reserved for dissenters.

So Communism, in rejecting God and His faith, has deprived itself of that last bulwark in which man found strength against fear, calamity, deprivation and oppression. Communist States, wherever established, have built an atmosphere of despotism, fear, terror and cruelty, turned men into flocks of timid sheep and goats and a herd of dumb-driven cattle that have been deprived of intention and free will. Thus, they have been deprived of those high ideals that are the goal of every dignified human society.

The Western Civilization's offshoots of Capitalism and Socialism have destroyed the peace and tranquillity of man and trampled upon his highest aims and objectives. The reason lies in the fact that this civilization made material prosperity its real target. Whoever failed to attain this goal became wretched. Even those who achieved this aim got nothing out of it except grief and dejection culminating in suicide.

The West has now started to realize its moral and spiritual

bankruptcy and many of its people are turning their eyes towards the East with the hope that they might possibly come across something in its religions and beliefs that may successfully fill their spiritual void. They hope that they may once again recuperate the human dignity that they have lost. Thus it is no astonishment that one notices in these countries, and particularly in America, many people converting to Buddhism, Bahaism, or Islam. Among them there are two groups that embrace Islam—one agreeing with Islam at the intellectual and ideological level and the other that is satisfied with it at the intuitive and spiritual level.

Once a new convert to Islam, Mr. Abu Bakr, a British Orientalist, told me the story of how he embraced Islam. He had been a professor of English language at the University of Fuad [now known as University of Cairo], and it was there that he embraced the religion of peace. He is at present the secretary of the Eastern section of the National Library, London. Explaining the reasons behind his opting for Islam, he said that Western Civilization had destroyed human dignity and the beauty of man's life. I said to him, 'Where the loss of human dignity is concerned, I won't question your opinion, but how did you come to the conclusion on the beauty of man's life? Western people have a very high opinion of the Western Civilization as regards beauty of the mode of living, that of habitation and beauty of the female sex—in short there is consideration for every type of aesthetic taste in it.' He said in reply, "This civilization has destroyed the beauty of the soul and intuition and morals."

During the summer of 1956, I delivered a lecture in a mosque in Paris. In keeping with the occasion of the birth of the Prophet ﷺ, I had spoken of the Islamic mission based on equity and justice and affection, and had pointed out that this attribute of Islam had been prominent even during the period of conquest and rule. I had also hinted at the greatest massacre of history in Algiers. After the lecture, among the people who were introduced to me was an Italian gentleman—a new convert to Islam by the name of Mustafa Wilson. He was the Italian Consul in Paris. On embracing Islam, he took leave of his diplomatic office. He is now at the head of a party of young French men who have sincerely taken to Islam, although at present his organization is little known—almost obscure. All these people gather once a week at their leader's home. All of them dress in a purely oriental fashion and some of them have grown a beard. In this weekly meeting, some portion of the Quran is recited and the Islamic faith is studied. Mustafa Wilson said to me, "I have carefully noted how you have stressed the aspect of mercy and compassion in the Islamic conquests. It is possible that you were refuting the totally false charge of Western writers that Muslims in their warfare had warranted cruelty and hard-heartedness? You should not be worried on that score. Every nation has a distinctive feature of its own on the moral plane which becomes its hallmark. The most outstanding feature of the morality of the Western nations is that they are absolutely hypocritical in all their assertions of mercy and affection."

An Arab Muslim was talking to these young French men on the theme of the greatness of Islam and its progressiveness. He got so carried away that it appeared he was speaking in some

Arab country on the subject of attainment of power and glory. So he stressed the point that Islam invites them to procure strength, to manufacture tanks, airplanes and the like. One of the converts to Islam said to him, "My brother! We have come from Western Civilization to Islam for the reason that this civilization has crippled our nerves through wars and armaments. Annihilating our souls and making our lusts abiding through materialism have put an end to our humanity. So you must only mention to us the spirituality of Islam in which we have sought human dignity and spiritual satisfaction."

Similarly, a Swiss girl, who lives in Paris and is studying Psychiatry, stated to me, 'I am a poor girl and my parents are not in a position to undertake my total support in this habitation of traders and libertines and fornicators. You must have observed that in this city man becomes a hungry beast of an evil nature. I thought of getting employment with some family to supplement my subsistence while working for my degree. So I looked for an oriental family in whose spiritual atmosphere my nobility and humanity would be safe. I got a part-time job with a Hindu family in Paris. However, I am sorry to say that I could find no trace of our lost assets there either. I discovered much to my grief that their souls also lacked nobility!'

These are some examples which tell of Western man's quest for spiritual life in which he may get rid of the tribulations of his materialistic civilization; distraction, helplessness, anxiety and restlessness; which are at the core of this civilization. One realizes this whenever talking to any person from the West with balanced thought and moral and spiritual consciousness.

Western civilization is the champion of materialistic life. However, material prosperity alone cannot lead man to peace and prosperity. Rather, man is in need of a civilization and culture in which, along with material progress, there is a drive for balanced spiritual growth. Neither of these two aspects of human life may overstep its limits, creating an unpleasant effect on the other. Is such a culture possible, and can it be brought into existence? Does a nation exist which can come forward to meet this challenge? It is not possible for the Western world to occupy this high position, since at present it is at the highest point of its material power and occupies the role of troublemaker. However, in days to come when its might gives way and decline sets in, it will be found sadly lacking in the capacity and capability to provide and keep intact the world leadership needed for the maintenance of peace, tranquillity, dignity and honor. As for the Socialist world, it is all the more difficult for it to discharge this duty since it is thoroughly steeped in materialism and has declared a war against spiritual, religious and moral values. The civilization based on Socialism along with the Western world will not be able to fill the spiritual and moral vacuum which its architects and citizens have now come to recognize.

Where the heathen and idolatrous religions of the East are concerned, they too cannot take upon themselves this responsibility, since civilization and culture must be founded upon strength of knowledge and a healthy ideology which is absolutely free from superstition and nonsensical whims. Idolatry in itself is the very opposite of all these things. Moreover, the civilization that the world demands and the spiritualism that it needs is such a positive and constructive spiritualism that it will be helpful in the progress and advancement of mankind. Thus, the duality of the East is a negative approach which prompts man to escapism, impedes the path of fulfilling rights and obligations and regards the material progress of man an abomination, making abstention from it and fighting against it obligatory. In the present age, the only one capable of playing this cultural role and becoming the standard-bearer of the civilization of the future is the Muslim *Ummah*. Below are the reasons for this proposition:

Firstly, Muslims are the bearers of a creed which is the most advanced in the matter of bringing into existence a civilization. This is the creed of an extremely pure, lucid, exalted, sublime and perfect unity of God. This creed respects intellect and gives it such strength that little known or less important facts are included in the category of information or knowledge. This is a moderate creed of highly dignified human morality which keeps man away from excess in mercy and affection and from deficiency in equity and justice. It establishes and maintains a balance between love and duty and its laws, which are founded upon wisdom and expediency, aim at liberalism and easiness rather than difficulty and hardship. In it the expediency of the individual is a guarantee for the collective expediencies, and expediency of the individual is not sacrificed to those of the collective or society. Human expediency in general is what is always kept in view, without destroying the national and regional characteristics and local preferences.

Secondly, Muslims are heirs to a positive and constructive spirituality. This is a divine spirituality accompanying each individual at all times. Rather than creating difficulties, it paves the path of excellence for the individual. This spirituality reminds him of God who created him from the earth on which he moves about, from humanity with whom he lives, from the unity of the universe of which he is a part and of God, the Cherisher of the Worlds.

Thirdly, Muslims have also proved in the past that they have the power of giving birth to such civilizations. Whatever might have been the adverse remarks of our antagonists and rejecters, no one dare deny the fact that Islamic Civilization had proved to bring more mercy and good fortune to mankind. Islamic Civilization proved to be the best ideal in the matter of superiority of morals, the rule of justice and equity, the freshness of the spirit, and in the various modes and periods of humanity. If Muslims were able to create such a wonderful human civilization in a period of much less enlightenment and backwardness in knowledge and thought, then they are today much better equipped and better placed with the advancement in knowledge, inventions and discoveries of the modern age to re-establish such a civilization.

When Muslims take the reins of this long awaited civilization in their hands, they will not make our flight into space an argument for the denial of God. They shall not make weapons and missiles to threaten the nations of the world and bring them into their sphere of influence. They shall not make women the means of the satisfaction of our lust. They shall not exploit and plunder the various nations of the world on the strength of the advancement of civilization, nor ruin their honor and wealth.

These are the reasons that have made Muslims a unique *Ummah*, which duly deserve to uphold the new civilization and put an end to the wretchedness of man, thus conferring on him peace, tranquillity and solace.

When Muslims contemplate the foundation of their creed, they find that their heavenly revelation is clearly pointing to the fact that they stand out among the nations of the world as a unique *Ummah* that can play the cultural role for mankind. This distinction is not based on race or sex, since Islam did not approve of these notions. Rather, it is based on the first two reasons presented in the following lines, *You are the best community that has been raised for mankind. You enjoin what is good and forbid what is evil, and you believe in Allah* (Quran, 3:110).

This Quranic verse points to the Muslim creed and morals which have made them the best *Ummah*. In another verse it has been said, *Those who, if We give them power in the earth, they establish Prayer and pay the Zakāt, and enjoin good and forbid evil* (Quran, 22:41).

In another place, the Quran states, *Thus have We made you a middle nation, so that you may be witness against mankind, and that the Messenger may be a witness against you* (Quran, 2:143). This Quranic verse has made Muslims the standard-bearer of a mission—to lead mankind and to always keep guiding them to the path of the truth and goodness. This obligation is not limited to any particular period or race.

When Muslims responded positively to the natural message and upheld this mission, they led humanity to the goal of peace, guidance and light. Then relinquishing the charge of this duty, they sought refuge in escape. This noble verse of the Quran pleads that Muslims enlighten the nations that are now groping in the darkness of distraction, selfishness, oppression, fatal despair and suicide and asks them to deliver them of their troubles. Individuals are putting an end to their lives with ordinary lethal weapons or poisoning themselves, whilst the nations are piling stocks of atomic and nuclear bombs for mass annihilation.

Regarding the new cultural role to be played by Muslims, there are two groups. The first group is enslaved by Western Civilization and has lost faith in its own nation. Thus, it feels that it can never come up to confront [the ideals of] Western people, not to speak of occupying the exalted position of leadership of the world. These are the countless troubles and perversions of thought with which the Muslim *Ummah* is confronted. This class of people in the Muslim *Ummah* is constantly dwindling numerically. The reason lies partly in the evils of the modern civilization and the crimes perpetrated against its followers and other weaker nations, and partly in the ideological and political awakening of the Muslim *Ummah* which answers well. The period of political slavery to Western Imperialism has come to an end and the rule of the political leaders of Muslims, who regarded the end of imperialism something impossible, is also coming to a close. In the same way the period of the cultural bondage of the "civilized" West will shortly come to an end, and Muslims shall also get rid of the conservative "enlightened and liberal" leaders, who were stupid, slavish and ignorant.

The second group of Muslims recognizes the endemic problems of Western Civilization and its excessive mischief and trouble making. However, like us they do not recognize the possibility of our laying the foundation of a movement for a modern civilization, when there is such a vast difference between the civilized nations and us. So all talk of cultural leadership appears to them idealistic and utopian.

From the beginning of our renaissance we have been through various stages, every later stage of which was the natural outcome of the preceding one. When we awakened we found ourselves badly entangled in the meshes of colonialism. We have turned out colonialists from most countries, and God-willing, will be able to drive them out of the rest in the near future. We have already started learning their manners and practices, and are organizing our lives according to the inevitable demands of the modern civilization. This is the same civilization which had, the day before, become the master of our destiny, and which had conquered our countries and dominated them. Then we went a step further on the way of attaining power. We exploited our natural resources and did our best to become independent of the West in manufacturing. Now, all our efforts are directed towards becoming members of the committee of the civilized nations and their partners in political power and economy. At this stage, it is essential for us to establish a norm of civilization in which both unique circumstances and need have been considered. Similarly, it is also necessary for us, before the conclusion of this stage, to prepare a plan of action for the coming stage. Shall we continue existing under this very civilization and chase after these people who are centuries ahead of us, so that helplessness and misery surround us on all sides?

Our aspirations are reduced to a merger with our predecessors on this path of action for ourselves which may serve to spur us on to further advances and also safeguard us against the difficulties, calamities, degradation and depression that have overtaken these civilized nations.

Realistically, we cannot reach the Western nations in material strength in a few years. Supposing we do acquire [their material strength] in a few years, then the West during this interval must have advanced ahead of us a great deal.

Thus, the right course to adopt would be to design a new cultural norm for ourselves and for the human race. The fact is that when choosing the pattern of civilization, we can have full freedom, and we have ample time at our disposal to consider the difficulties and hazards of the present day civilization. The reason for adopting such a course is not only that in the present stage we could get rid of the hold of this civilization on us, since there is no other way of doing that, but also that our real aim is to get free of the evil elements and immunize ourselves against it at some stage in the future. The way of achieving this goal is clear for us provided we have a staunch belief in our principles and faith, and have certainty about those values whose accuracy and truth have been proved by experience and which lie at the foundations of our civilization. The spark of temerity and exaltation in our great nation has not yet died down and the fires of daring and passion, of sacrificing for a noble cause have not yet been extinguished. In spite of receiving constant wounds from the invaders and occupying forces and putting up with the strokes from the internal traitors, we have never yielded to the perpetrators of oppression and tyranny.

If we achieve this end we will find that we have guided the modern period of human history in the most important direction. In this way, we shall be able to put the stamp of our spiritual and moral authority over the continents of Asia and Africa, which will make them more fortunate and deserving of peace and security. At this point, the West will need to turn to us and acquire from us the lessons and guidance that will lessen its poor condition and affliction. That will be the day when leadership will change hands and Muslims shall be the leaders, and before some people in their moments of insanity put an end to the human race, Muslims shall have succeeded in guiding humanity in another direction.

It occurs to me time and again that the trend of historical incidents is not in keeping with the sequence of events that thinkers and writers have taken into their minds. Who knows what may happen tomorrow? This world is full of unpredicted events. Something happens at one end of the globe and has a deep impact on those living at the other end. However, it does not prevent us from contemplating the future. Events of history are planned by Allah through the views of the thinkers and the call of the prophets and reformers.

This book is a collection of talks that I delivered and which were broadcast on Radio Damascus between September 8 and December 15, 1955. In these talks, I had presented some of the unique aspects of Islamic Civilization, aspects that would fascinate every man of thought and vision. I have not undertaken an exhaustive study of these cultural manifestations, nor did I try to analyse them academically, since I was addressing people whose intellectual levels were different. My aim in delivering these speeches was to make people listen and adopt the best of what I have said, particularly the youth and thinkers who believe and have faith in their history. However, I could not continue this series of talks, since I was preparing for an academic tour of the Western countries, which I completed in 1956. I had in mind to present many more of unique examples—examples of humanity in our cultural history from which positive spirituality radiates, examples of belief in God, pursuit of Truth, chastity of psyche, illumination of soul, beauty of character, sympathy for mankind and just and equitable rule. All this was in spite of fact that they fully participated in all the tumultuous events of the culture and civilization and were all the time very actively busy in the arena of life. Furthermore, this vast multitude includes rulers, learned men in the religious lore, philosophers and leaders, traders and officials, men and women, young and old and prosperous and the needy alike. They were not the visionary ideals of the imaginary world of the philosophers and intellectuals, but specimens of human excellence that lived with the people on this earth.

So captivating are these examples of positive spirituality that Islamic Civilization stands out unique among all the old and the new civilizations. True, history is acquainted with some spiritual figures who were born in various nations, particularly in the Far East, and even today there are people who are dominated by a chaste trend of spirituality. However, all such personalities had an individualistic and negative approach to civilization. They hated the bustle of life and tried to escape culture and civilization. They exist in temples, mountains, caves and in the wilderness. But the men of Islamic history are those who entered the thick of the struggle in the arena of life and mended and adorned it. In striving to reform and making life more pleasant for people, they offered unflinching sacrifice of life and property that was needed for this purpose. This is the real secret of the unparalleled beauty of the amazing spiritual men in the history of civilizations.

The aim in the publication of these radio talks is to draw attention to these unique aspects, whose presence is a strong argument in support of the fact that Muslims have and had the capability of establishing a civilization that is superior and more perfect than the present one. It also serves to remind the younger generation of the Muslim *Ummah* of the need to establish such an exalted civilization the way it was founded by their ancestors. This is the most appropriate time for such a reminder since the Muslim *Ummah* is stepping into a new era with great enthusiasm and fervour and it possesses the ability to build a better and superior future. The Muslim *Ummah* still retains the habits, disposition and talents of the ancestors. Thus when Muslims hear the stories of the excellence, eminence and respectability of their ancestors, they are motivated into constructive work.

In presenting these lectures, it was never my intention to assert that each and every thing in Islamic history was beautiful and bright. There is no civilization in history whose standard-bearers were entirely free of mistakes. What is intended is to establish that the unique humanitarian aspects of Islamic

Civilization were stronger and more beautiful. It aims to refute the charges of those critics who only find faults and defects in Islamic Civilization and who try to remove Islamic Civilization from the history of lasting and well established civilizations of the world. It aims to defeat the endeavours to conceal from the view of the young generation the historical impressions and traditions of Islamic Civilization, so that they may drown the fervour of the young generation along with themselves.

I have presented only a few specimens of the glorious Islamic Civilization. I hope that those making a historical study of Islamic Civilization shall take it to completion in great detail and full elucidation. In this way, it may appear before the young generation in its proper attractive form and with perfect grace and beauty. The nation that remains ignorant and unaware of its history, in spite of having a glorious past, has no present either. The nation that remains elevated from its unique characteristics and excellences, has no future, since every nation and civilization has a national relationship with its past and it is its fundamental characteristics that bring civilization into existence. Those passing sarcastic remarks like, "It is the favorite pastime of the idle and the good-for-nothing to get acquainted with the past and to go on mourning for it," forget the fact that to ignore and deride the past is the way of the ignorant and malicious people. Our prosperity lies in our benefiting from our treasure houses of the past in the construction of our present, so that our growth and ascent may have a happy end; that our future may be prosperous and the means of the survival of the Muslim *Ummah* may be part and parcel of all endeavours in this direction. In this way, past honor and excellences derived from our ancestors, together with the future greatness, may become one. Thus our caravan shall retain its continuity on the path of history; the links of the past and those of the future shall be joined and become continuous and we shall advance towards perfection.

The fact is that the completion of any work depends on the Will of Allah, and it is His Graciousness and Help that is needed in everything we do.

Mustafa Sibaʿī

CHAPTER ONE

CHARACTERISTICS OF ISLAMIC CIVILIZATION

SOME AUTHORS HAVE defined civilization as "a collective system which helps man in increasing his cultural production." Civilization is composed of four fundamental elements: economic means, political system, moral principles and the pursuit of sciences and arts. For the continuity and development of a civilization there are certain geographical, economic and psychological factors, such as faith, language, education and training. Similarly, for the downfall of a civilization there are certain factors that are the opposite of those factors which establish it and develop it. Some of the factors amongst these are moral and ideological disintegration, disruption of law and order, spread of oppression and poverty, spread of pessimism and indifference and loss of sincere and capable leaders.

The story of civilization begins from the time when humans were known and it is an inter-connected link that civilized nations pass on to the one after it, not specific to any land or race, based rather on the above mentioned factors. There has perhaps, never been a nation which has not made additions to the pages of the history of civilization. However, what distinguishes one civilization from another is the strength of the foundations upon which it is based, the strong influence that it has, and the universal goodness that it has conferred to humanity because of its establishment. The more universal the civilization is in its message, humanistic in its attitude, moral in its direction and realistic in its principles, the more lasting in history and the more immortal and respectable it will be regarded.

Islamic Civilization is also a link in the chain of human civilizations. Many civilizations have preceded it, and many more shall follow it. There were many factors responsible for the establishment of Islamic Civilization and certain causes for its downfall. However, those factors and causes are outside the scope of this discourse, since we have limited ourselves to discuss the important role of Islamic Civilization in the history of human advancement and the extent to which it contributed in the field of theology, science, morals, wisdom, art, and literature.

The most outstanding aspects that attracts a person studying Islamic Civilization are the following characteristics.

1. Unity of God

Islamic Civilization rests on the foundation of the creed of the Unity of God. It is the first civilization to call for the worship of One God who has no partner in His Sovereignty and Rule. Only He must be worshipped, and He alone must be taken as the aim [in life], and refuge must be sought in Him alone: *You do we worship, and Your help we seek* (Quran, 1:4). It is He who gives power and humiliates, gives and grants. There is nothing between the heaven and the earth that is not under His Power and in His Grip.

This nobility or loftiness in understanding the Unity of God had a huge influence in elevating the position of man and freeing the common people from the tyranny of kings, the noble people, the mighty and of the people of religion. It also had an influence in rectifying the relationship between the ruler and the ruled and focusing the vision on Allah alone, who is the Creator of creation and the Lord of the worlds. This creed had such a profound influence on Islamic Civilization that it stood out among all the former civilizations of the world. It became free from every phenomenon and philosophy of paganism in its creed, governance and in its arts, poetry and literature. This is why Muslims have abstained from translating *Iliad* and other heathen pieces of Greek literature. In spite of being experts in architecture, mosaics, engraving, painting and other types of decorative arts, they did not venture into the field of portrait painting and idol making. Islam, which had openly declared a war against paganism and its manifestations, did not permit its civilization to make statues of the leaders, the virtuous, the prophets and the conquerors. In other civilizations statues were viewed as the most outstanding phenomena, since none of these civilizations had attained the position of Islam in the creed of the Unity of God.

This creed of the Unity of God [*tawḥīd*] was the basis and foundation of Islamic Civilization. There was such great unity in the message, unity in legislation, unity in the enterprises relating to the masses, unity in the general human essence, unity in the means of subsistence, unity in the pattern of thought, that those studying the Islamic Arts have observed the unity of style and taste in different works of art. A piece of Andalusian ivory, another piece from Egyptian fabric, a third piece from Syrian pottery and the fourth, a jewelry created from Persian minerals, appear to be of the same kind and bear the same stamp [of the *tawḥīd* culture] despite its variance of shape and design.

2. Humanitarian and Universal

The second characteristic of Islamic Civilization is its humanitarian attitude, its aim and the universality of its horizon and message. The Quran had declared the unity of mankind in spite of the variety of race, family and homeland: *O mankind! We created you from a single [pair] of a male and a female, and made you into nations and tribes so that you may know each other. Verily the most honored of you in the sight of Allah is [one who is] the most God-fearing of you* (Quran, 49:13).

When the Quran declared this universal unity of mankind on truth, goodness and honor, it made its civilization join together all geniuses of the peoples and nations conquered by Islam. That is why every other civilization except Islamic Civilization can take pride in the geniuses of only one race and one nation. It can take pride in all the genius sons of all those nations and tribes who had joined hands in building the edifice of Islamic Civilization: Abū Ḥanīfah, Mālik, al-Shāfiʿī, Aḥmad, al-Khalīl, al-Sībawayh, al-Kindi, al-Ghazālī, al-Fara, al-Farābī, Ibn Rushd and many other renowned men. In spite of their different origins and regional affiliations, they are an example of the geniuses that Islamic Civilization has presented to humanity and the best production of sound human thought.

3. Priority of Moral Principles

The third characteristic of Islamic Civilization is that it has assigned as top priority the moral principles in its entire system and all its activities. It has never lost sight of these principles and has never made them the means of the material benefits for rulers, groups or individuals. Application of the moral principles has always been kept in view in governance, learning, arts, legislation, peace, war, economy and in familial affairs. Rather, the height of perfection and excellence attained by Islamic Civilization in this regard has never been reached by any other old or new civilization. The traces and impressions left by Islamic Civilization in this field are marvellous. Rather, this is the one and only civilization which has guaranteed only prosperity and good fortune for mankind such that no suffering or distress contaminated it.

4. Intellect and Heart

The fourth characteristic is that this civilization has faith in the true principles of knowledge and makes the chaste principles and the tenets of belief its nucleus. It has addressed the intellect [thought] and the heart [sentiments] simultaneously and thus stands out among other civilizations that are unable to match this. This amazing characteristic has enabled Islamic Civilization to create a system of governance built upon the principles of truth and justice, focusing on faith and belief without their being any impediment in the growth and development of the State and the civilization. Rather, the faith is the most important factor in its development. The radiation of knowledge emanating from the mosques of Baghdad, Damascus, Cordoba and Granada had enlightened all parts of the world without exception. Islamic Civilization is the only civilization that does not separate religion from the state. However, in spite of this intimate combination of the two, it never experienced any of the evils which had overtaken Europe during the Middle Ages. The head of the Islamic State was the Caliph and Amīr of Muslims. The rule was not in his own right, rather for the establishment and maintenance of the Truth. Legislation was for the specialists and every group of scholars in their field of specialization was equal before the law. Excellence and superiority was based on piety and the extent of service to mankind. A woman by the name of Fāṭimah was brought before the law for theft, and when intercession on her behalf was sought, the Messenger of Allah said, "By Allah! If Fāṭimah bint Muḥammad [Fāṭimah, the daughter of Muḥammad] had been found guilty of theft, I would have cut off her hand!" (Bukhārī and Muslim). Once the Prophet ﷺ said, "All of mankind is the family of Allah. So the most beloved to Allah is he who is the most beneficent to His children." (Bazzār). This is the faith upon which our civilization is founded and there is no distinction or special privilege for any ruler, religious person, any aristocrat or wealthy person: *Say: "I am but a man like yourselves"* (Quran, 18:110).

5. Religious Tolerance

The final remarkable characteristic of Islamic Civilization is its marvellous religious tolerance which has never been witnessed in a civilization based on religious foundations. However, it is possible for one not reposing faith in God and any known [revealed] faith to regard all religions as equally respectable and treat its followers on an equal footing.

However, the follower of a faith who is convinced that his faith is true and his creed is the truest and most accurate is then afforded a chance of lifting the sword, conquering lands, and ruling and sitting in judgment over them; and even then his faith and belief do not allow him to be a tyrant in his rule, to pervert the administration of justice and to compel people to enter the fold of his own faith. Such a person would be regarded as extraordinary. Therefore, how extraordinary and unique would it be if there was an entire civilization founded on a religious basis and built on these principles, but in spite of all that, it had adopted the behavior of utmost tolerance, justice, mercy and humanity? This feat was accomplished by Islamic Civilization, and many examples of this will be presented. It is enough for us to learn that Islamic Civilization is unique in this regard, that it established only one faith, but its blessings benefited all other religions.

These are some of the characteristics of Islamic Civilization and its uniqueness in history which has astonished the world, and which was the cause of attraction for the serious and intelligent people of every faith and race. That was the time when this civilization was strong and in power, directing men towards the good, refining morals and educating the world. However, when this civilization was on the decline and another civilization took birth, there were some differences of opinion about the worth of our civilization. Some looked down upon it and others praised it. One man recounted its merits and excellence and another exaggerated its faults. Western researchers are divided in their opinions about Islamic Civilization and are not competent to arbitrate and sit in judgment on Islamic Civilization. They hold the norms of judgment of these days and their opinions are accepted since they hold sway over the world and the reins of civilization are in their hands. The people and civilizations on whom they are pronouncing judgments are so infirm that the powerful nations have covetously fixed their gazes on them so that what little remains with them may be snatched away as they pander to their desire for power and their avarice. Perhaps this is the stand taken by the strong against the weak that the former disdains and finds faults with him. That is what the mighty have done with the helpless in every age, with Islamic Civilization being the only exception. When it was powerful, it dealt justly with both the strong and the weak, and recognized excellence wherever it existed whether in the East or the West. Who can match Islamic Civilization in the matter of just rule, the purity of objectives and consistency of conscience in the history of the world?

It is regrettable that we are not aware of the prejudice of the powerful nations of the world and their unjust opinion about Islamic Civilization. Many of them are blindfolded by religious bigotry and are unable to witness the truth. Also, national prejudice at work in them does not allow them to recognize the excellence of any other nation. The fact that we ourselves are influenced by their opinions of us is not understandable. We are unable to understand why some individuals of our own nation look derisively at this civilization, which is their own, and at whose feet the whole world has bowed down for centuries.

Perhaps the argument of those who do not hold Islamic Civilization in such high regard is this: in comparison with the inventions and conquests in the practical field of the modern civilization, Islamic Civilization stands nowhere. However, even if this assertion is accurate, it does not lower the dignity and exalted position of Islamic Civilization on two accounts.

First, every civilization comprises two elements, a moral (or spiritual) element and a material element. Where the material element is concerned, the succeeding civilization undoubtedly has superiority over the preceding one. This evolution in life and its resources is in accordance with the Divine law, and one cannot expect the preceding civilization to have all that the succeeding one has acquired in this regard. If this had been justifiable we would have been justified in looking down upon all those civilization preceding Islamic Civilization since it also had invented such resources of life and phenomena of civilization of which the preceding civilization had no trace. So the material element is not the true basis for the determination of any lasting and abiding excellence among the various civilizations.

As for the moral and spiritual element, it is this that makes any civilization immortal and through which humanity acquires good fortune and is safeguarded against all hazards and grief.

In this field, Islamic Civilization has left behind both the preceding and the succeeding ones and has attained a stage of evolution unparalleled in the history of cultures and civilizations. This one fact is enough to make Islamic history everlasting. The real purpose of a civilization is that man may attain the height of blessings and good fortune, and the service that Islamic Civilization has rendered towards this end has not been achieved by any other civilization in the East or the West.

Second, civilizations should not be compared on the strength of material standard nor by the number of monuments or the material luxury in living standards. Rather, it should be compared by means of the remnants which it has left for humanity. The same is true of wars and empires. They too are not compared on the basis of the area of their empires or the number of fighting men that took part in any war. If the wars waged during the distant past and the Middle Ages are compared with the Second World War in the matter of the number of fighting forces and the military hardware, the former pale in significance. But those old wars have great importance and historical significance, since they have resulted in far-reaching effects on the history of mankind. The battle at Caunae [Italy, 216 BC], in which the world-renowned Carthaginian general, Hannibal, had badly defeated the Romans, is still taught today in the military schools of Europe.

The great feats of Khālid ibn al-Walīd in the conquests of Iraq and Syria are still studied by Western experts of warfare, and they still marvel at it. These wars are the brightest chapters of our wars and conquests. The battles of Caunae, Badr, Qādisiyyah and Hittin cannot be lost sight of just because they belong to the distant past, for they are milestones in the history of mankind.

After this brief discourse, I am sure the eyes must have been lifted to witness the beautiful manifestations of Islamic Civilization. What is to follow is a description of some of the fascinating aspects of that Islamic Civilization.

CHAPTER TWO

HISTORICAL IMPRESSIONS OF ISLAMIC CIVILIZATION

ISLAMIC CIVILIZATION HAS played a magnificent role in the history of human development and has left far-reaching effects in the field of belief, knowledge, governance, philosophy, arts and literature. The unique historical impressions of Islamic Civilization can be discussed under five main categories:

1. Creed and Faith

The principles of Islamic Civilization have left a very deep impression on the religious reformist movements that have been established in Europe from the seventh century to modern times. Islam is that faith that imparted the lesson of the Unity of God and that He has no partners in His Sovereignty and Authority. It taught that God is free from anthropomorphism, injustice, tyranny, defects and shortcomings. Islam has also made it very clear that man in his devotional acts, in strengthening his relationship with God and to understand the Divine Laws, does not stand in need of the mediation of priests or the clergy and such other classes. In opening up the minds of nations and guiding them to these firm principles, Islam has acted as a powerful factor. Prior to the advent of Islam, the nations of the world were in the strong grip of the most violent kind of religious despotism and leadership that had held their thought and opinion incarcerated; in fact, their bodies and their goods were in its possession. It was the natural consequence of the conquests of Islam in the East and West that the nations around the lands directly under the Islamic rule became influenced by the creed and ideology of Islam. That was what actually happened. In the seventh century of the Christian era many reformers arose in Europe who were against polytheism. In later times, there arose such people who refused to take men as the mediators between God and His servants and invited people to understand the holy books independent of the clergy and the Pope.

Many researchers have vehemently asserted that Martin Luther [1483-1546, leader of the Protestant Reformation in Germany] was influenced in his reformation movement by the Arab philosophers and Muslim scholars in the field of faith, creed and revelation. The European universities at that time used to depend on the books written by Muslim philosophers that had been translated into Latin. The movement for the separation of the church and the state, which was announced during the French Revolution, was the product of those powerful ideological movements which pervaded Europe for over three hundred years. Islamic Civilization had influenced these movements through contact with the Crusades and through Muslim rule in Andalusia.

2. Philosophy and Science

In the fields of Medicine, Mathematics, Chemistry, Geography and Astronomy, Islamic Civilization left historical impressions. The awakening in the field of learning in Europe was the result of the instruction that the Europeans had received as students of Muslim scholars and philosophers in Isabella, Cordoba and Granada. When the students from the West came to these education centres, they were amazed to find that the doors of these sciences and arts were open to every person and that everyone could benefit from them, devoting himself to them with great enthusiasm and concentration in a free atmosphere, since there was no parallel in their own land. At the time the Muslim scholars were working on their lectures and on their compilations, the minds of the Europeans were filled with nonsensical ideas about scientific facts, like the revolution of the earth and its spherical shape and the movements of the heavenly bodies. It was here that the movement of rendering Arabic texts into Latin started, and the books written by the Muslim scholars were being taught in the European educational institutions. *Al-Qānūn* on the theme of Medicine by Ibn Sīna was translated in the twelfth century. Al-Rāzī's *al-Hawī,* which is much more voluminous than the *al-Qānūn,* was translated around the end of the thirteenth century. Up to the sixteenth century, Europe depended on these materials on Medical Science from the Arab sources for their teaching and practice of Medicine. Where the profuse literature on philosophy is concerned, its teaching continued there even longer, and Europe became acquainted with

Greek philosophy through these compilations and translations. This is why many European writers confess that during the Middle Ages the Muslim scholars were the teachers and instructors of Europe for at least six centuries.

The learned author, Gustav Lebon says, "For five to six hundred years, general books in Arabic language and particularly on various disciplines have been almost the only source of learning and teaching in the European universities. We can safely assert that in certain disciplines like Medicine the impressions of the Arabs are still at work in Europe. The Medical writings of Ibn Sīna have been explained about the close of the last century in Monabiliah." The same author further says, "Roger Bacon, Leonard, Erno al-Felquni, Raymond Lot, San Thoma, Albert and Azfonish Qashqani have solely depended on Arabic books."

Monsieur Renan says, "Albert the Great is indebted to Ibn Sīna, and San Thoma owes it all to Ibn Rushd." The famous orientalist Sideo writes, "During the Middle Ages, the Arabs alone were the standard-bearers of a civilization." The barbarism of Europe, which had been ravaged during the onslaughts of the Northern tribes, had been removed by the Arabs alone. The Arabs gained access to ancient Greek philosophy and not contented with acquiring this knowledge, extended its scope vastly and opened up new avenues for the study of the universe. The learned author also says, "When the Arabs gained expertise in Astronomy, they paid special attention to Mathematical Sciences and gained a high degree of excellence and they were really our teachers in this field." He says that when one takes stock of all that was transferred from Arabic to Latin, one finds that a great doorway was made in the name of Gerbert Salifster II during the period between 970–980 CE, in which all those sciences he had acquired in Andalusia had entered Europe.

The learned English author O'Hallard toured Andalusia and Egypt some time between 1100 and 1200 CE and translated from Arabic *al-Arkān* by Euclid, which had been unknown to the West until then. Another learned person, Plato Taiguli, translated *al-Akar* by Theodosius from its Arabic version. Rudu Brugie translated from Arabic Ptolemy's book on *Geography of the Inhabited Earth*. Leonard Baige, wrote out, around 1200 CE, a treatise on Algebra which he had picked up from his Arab teachers. Kunbanos Nausy has done the best translation of the Arabic text of Euclid during the thirteenth century. Also Fastaloon of Bologna, drawing upon Ḥasan ibn Haytham's book *al-Baṣariyyāt,* propagated the astronomical science in the West. In 1250 CE, Aznofish Qashqani ordered the publication of an astronomical almanac which took its name from him. During this period, on the one side, Roger I ordered the study of Arabic sciences and arts, particularly those written by Idrīsī, and, on the other, Frederick II highly stressed the learning of sciences and manners. The sons of Ibn Rushd were always with him at the court and taught him the natural history of the plants and animals.

Homeld writes in his book on Science, "It was the Arabs who for the first time invented the method of the chemical preparation of medicines, and it was from this source that sound advice and the procedure of experiments came to us. They were then taken up by the School of Saftram and spread to Southern Europe from there. Then the medicinal and natural elements on which medication entirely depends became the cause of the study of plants. In this way, both these studies went on simultaneously in two different ways, and thus the Arabs opened the door to a new era of the study of this science. It is sufficient proof for this assertion to realize the vastness of Arab knowledge of the plant kingdom and that they made an addition of two thousand herbs to those of Zulefuredas. There were many herbs in their pharmacy that the Greeks had not even dreamt of."

Sideo says about Rāzī and Ibn Sīna that both of them pervaded the educational institutions throughout Europe for a long time—particularly Ibn Sīna, who was introduced to Europe as a physician. For six hundred years his works were the reference points in the educational institutions of Europe. His book *al-Qānūn* [*Canon*] was translated in five volumes and had repeated reprints since the instruction in the universities of France and Italy totally depended on it.

3. Language and Literature

Western people and particularly the Spanish poets have been very much influenced by Arabic literature, horsemanship, chivalry and metaphor. Refined and unique topics found their way into Western literature through the activity of Arabic writers in Andalusia. The famous Spanish writer Abanese writes, "Before the entry of the Arabs into Spain and the spread of their stables, horses and horsemen throughout Southern Europe, horsemanship and chivalry were unknown in Europe." In the book written by Dousie on the topic of Islam, he quoted a letter of Algharu, a Spanish writer, who lamented the indifference of the Europeans to Latin and their attachment to the Arabic language. This shows that in those days the Western men of letters were very much impressed with Arabic learning and literature.

He says, "The intelligent people and men of tastes have been bewitched by the Arabic lyrics. So they looked down upon Latin and, leaving aside other languages, communicate in the official language. A contemporary surging with patriotic zeal has regretfully stated that his Christian brethren have been fascinated by the Arabic lyrical poetry and tales, and they study the books written by Muslim philosophers and legists. They do not study them to prove them wrong or to refute them but to pick up eloquent Arabic style. Who else, except the clergy, studies the commentaries on the Old and the New Testaments? Who is there to recite the gospels and the books of the prophets and the apostles? Alas! The younger generation with the new trends of thought does not look approvingly at any except the Arabic language and literature. They derive light of guidance from the books written by the Arabs, establish libraries comprising these books and sing praises of the Arabic treasures of learning and literature everywhere. When they hear of the Christian literature, they scowl and argue that it is not worth their time and attention. Alas! The Christians have forgotten their own language. You will not be able to find one in a thousand who writes letters to his friends in his own tongue. On the other hand, where Arabic is concerned, there are many who express themselves in its best style and write poetry in it which may excel even that written by Arabs in accuracy of idiom and eloquence."

During the fourteenth century and later, there have been many renowned men of letters whose literary writings and style bear the lasting impress of Arabic literature. In 1349 CE, the Italian novelist and poet Boccaccio wrote stories under the title *Ten Morns* [Deca Meron], in which the style of the world-renowned stories, *The Arabian Nights*, has been imitated. Shakespeare has derived the theme of one of his plays from this source. The German playwright Lissing has borrowed the plot of his drama *Natan the Physician* from the same source.

Chaucer (1340-1400), the father of modern English poetry, has mostly drawn upon Boccaccio. They had met in Italy, and afterwards he wrote his *Canterbury Tales*. Similar is the case with the famous poem of Dante, (1265-1321) *Divina Comedia* in which he has recounted the tales of his journey to the other world.

It has been said that Dante, at the time of writing this poem, had on his mind deep impressions of the treatise *Ghufrān* by Abū al-Ala al-Mu'arra and all that Ibn ʿArabī has written about the Genii. This is because he had lived in Sicily during the rule of Emperor Frederick II. This monarch was fond of cultural pursuits and pastimes, and studied cultural literature in the Arabic language. He used to have discussions with Dante on the Aristotelian theories the sources of which information came from the Arabic books. Dante was acquainted with the life of the Prophet Muḥammad ﷺ, the details of the Ascent of the Prophet and the accounts of the Heavens furnished by the prophetic traditions.

The period of Peter of York's life corresponds to the period when Arabian culture held sway over France and Italy. He had been educated at the Universities of Monabliyyah and Paris. Both of these Universities had been founded by scholars who had received instruction and training at the Andalusian Universities. Many books compiled by the Arab authors were taught there and the stories rife among the Arabs during the Middle Ages had a deep impact on Europe during the Renaissance. These include stories of chivalry and horsemanship and other feats of strength and valour that the renowned Arabs had performed for the sake of love and magnificence. In this connection, the translation of *The Arabian Nights* into European languages had a profound effect on European fiction. More than three hundred editions of this book had been published in several European languages. Several critics of Europe are of the opinion that the travelogue by Swift and Defoe's *Robinson Crusoe* are both indebted to *The Arabian Nights* and *Ḥayy ibn Nafīdhan* by the Arab philosopher Ibn Ṭufayl. Nobody can entertain any doubts about the fact that the repeated publication of *The Arabian Nights* reveals that the Europeans have made it the centre of their attention and have been very much influenced by it.

In various European languages, many Arabic words relating to the necessities of life are used in almost their original form. For example, cotton, musk, lemon, zero are Arabic words, and there are innumerable other words of that sort. Without going into detail, it would suffice to quote Mr. Michael, "Europe for its finest literature is indebted to the Arab countries. Similarly, the spiritual and ideological revolution during the Middle Ages had certain forces at work at its back, and the Arab nation had a great deal to do with putting them into action."

4. Legislation

The European students who were being educated in the educational institutions of Andalusia translated the Muslim literature on *Fiqh* and enforcement of the *Sharīʿah*. Europe at this time had no firm political system, nor were there any laws based on equity and justice. When Napoleon conquered Egypt, the well-known compendiums of *Fiqh* of the Mālikite School were translated into French. To begin with, *Kitāb Khalīl* was translated, which served as the basis for French Law. Thus one finds that the French Law of that period resembled to a great extent the *Fiqh* of the Mālikite School. Sideo says, "Our searching gaze rests on the Mālikite Law, since we have had contacts with Africa, and France had ordered its competent learned men to translate the short compendium on *Fiqh* compiled by Isḥāq ibn Yaʿqūb [d. 1422 CE] into French."

5. State and Government

In ancient times and even during the Middle Ages the right of the common people to call their rulers to account was not recognized. The relationship of the ruler and the ruled was that of the master and the slave. The ruler was a despot and treated the people as he pleased. The dominion was regarded as inheritance. This happened even if a princess inherited the throne and then married a ruler in an alien kingdom, and the two countries found themselves in a war for their shares in the land of the princess.

Again, when two kingdoms were engaged in a war, the conqueror came in possession of not only the conquered land but also the lives, property, honor, dignity and freedom of the vanquished people. These conditions and those propagated by it lasted until the era of Islamic Civilization dawned and became dominant. Islamic Civilization declared that people have a right to criticize and call to account their rulers, and that the latter are only the trustees and employees whose duty is to honestly guard the interests of the people. So for the first time in the history of the world, the citizens publicly asked the ruler to even account for the dress he was wearing. The ruler neither condemned him to be hanged for that offence nor imprisoned nor exiled him. On the contrary, the ruler explained his position and rendered account of the cloth that went into his mantle, which satisfied the objector and the rest of the assembly.

It also happened for the first time in the history of mankind that an individual from the common people addressed the ruler thus, "Peace be on you, O employee!" The ruler acknowledged that he was certainly an employee and hence it was his duty to serve the nation sincerely and to render his due relating to this trust. Islamic Civilization declared this principle and demonstrated its application and enforcement.

It was this spirit of the freedom of thought and conscience which was infused into all the nations that existed around the Islamic society. All these nations took turns to become dynamic, prepared themselves for a revolution, and at last broke their chains and became free. This process was then repeated throughout Europe. During the Crusades the Europeans entered Syria. Before this, in the Caliphate of Andalusia they had witnessed the people keeping a strict watch over their rulers and that they were responsible to their own people and not to any one else. The European rulers observed that Muslims and their rulers, instead of being subservient to any particular individual or class, were accountable to the entire nation. In contrast, the Roman Emperor dominated them, such that, unless they were to recognize the religious dominion of Rome, they faced failure and disappointment. So when these rulers returned to their own lands, they rebelled against Roman authority and finally became free. Consequently, the people of these lands rose in revolt against these monarchs and broke the shackles, becoming free. The French Revolution came much later and did not declare any other principle other than that which had been declared by Islamic Civilization twelve hundred years earlier.

Among the principles that Islamic Civilization had declared is that treaties must be respected; there must be complete freedom in the matter of creed, and the places of worship must be allowed to remain in the possession and under control of those worshipping in them. The personal freedom, honor and dignity of people should not be violated. It was the observance of this principle that helped create a spirit of dignity and self-respect in them, awakening the basic traits of nobility and humanity. So, history witnessed for the first time the scene when a non-Muslim complained to the head of the Islamic State that the son of his governor had flogged his son. The head of the State became infuriated on hearing this complaint and called the governor's son to account, and he was then flogged by the one who was originally wronged. Then he scolded the culprit's father saying, "Since when have you enslaved them when their mothers had borne them free?"

This was the new spirit that Islamic Civilization infused in the nations and the individuals. Had it been in any other civilization, the father who boldly took his grievance to the leader seeking redress would have been mercilessly beaten, his possessions plundered, and forced into the religion of the leadership. But the advent of Islamic Rule and Civilization redeemed him. Regarding rebellion, he dared not stand in protest or express grief on being oppressed. Rather, a sense of self-respect was lacking in him. When the sun of Islamic Civilization rose on him, his voice was raised and addressing the Leader of the Believers, he said, "I seek refuge in Allah against your oppression." What was this oppression? It was neither bloodshed, nor violation of chastity, nor compulsion in the matter of faith, nor confiscation of property. It was a minor issue of one boy having given another boy a few lashes.

The West was introduced to Islamic Civilization through Greater Syria [including modern Syria and Palestine] and Andalusia during the Middle Ages. Before this, the monarch dared not say a word against the religious leaders and the people against the monarchs. They lacked a sense and knowledge of the fact that calling the ruler to account or the support of the oppressed is their basic right. They were used to slaughtering each other like butchers slaughtering goats on the basis of the difference in creed. When they came in contact with Muslims, the sentiment of awakening and freedom was created in them and this enabled them to obtain liberty. Is it possible even after all this to deny the part played by Muslims in attaining liberty, humanity and freedom of action?

These are some of the everlasting traces of Islamic Civilization in five different major areas of life and in the life of nations and civilization. Muslims can justly assert that the nations in whom Islamic Civilization has infused the spirit of liberation from slavery are indebted to them. Yet Muslims would not like to square this deal by false boasts of past glory and nursing equally false hopes and longings. All that they want is that they may be able to create self-recognition in themselves so that they may become aware of the worth of their civilization and the importance of their inheritance. Once again, they may then create in themselves the capability of becoming the *Best Nation*, which will discharge the duty of being witness to the truth and will show humanity the way to goodness, truth and nobility.

CHAPTER THREE

PHILANTHROPY

IT IS NOT possible for a person discussing the impressions of the Islamic Civilization to lose sight of the human concern that distinguishes it from other civilizations. It transformed for humanity an atmosphere of hatred, malice, disunity and fanaticism to an atmosphere of love, tolerance, cooperation and equality in front of Allah. In the law and social fabric of the society, there was equality and no room for superiority of one race, group or nation over another. This concern for humanity was the basis of the principles of Islamic Civilization's laws and reality.

Where the Islamic principles and elements are concerned, it has declared that all of mankind has been created from one soul. The Quran says, *O mankind! Fear your Lord who created you from a single person [Adam] and from him He created his wife [Ḥawā] and from them both He created many men and women* (Quran, 4:1).

So humanity comes from the same origin and whatever it has later been divided into in terms of nations, tribes, countries, and races is merely the division of one house in which the brothers are from the same father and the same mother. Thus, the variations of races and nations should only be a means of co-operation and mutual recognition in good deeds. The Quran says, *O mankind! We created you from a single [pair] of a male and female, and made you into nations and tribes, that you may know each other* (Quran, 49:13).

Subsequently some individuals advance in life and others lag behind. Some become prosperous and others indigent. An individual becomes the ruler and a nation becomes subjugated. Some are white skinned and others are black. All this is in accordance with the natural laws and the unchanging systems of life. However, it certainly does not mean that these discrepancies should be allowed to become the cause of distinctions and dissensions between the prosperous and the humble, the rich and the poor and the ruler and the ruled or even between white and black. Rather, all are the same and equal and there is no distinction in the eyes of Allah except the one with *taqwā*. The Quran says, *Verily the most honored of you in the sight of Allah is [one who is] the most God-fearing of you* (Quran, 49:13). They are all equal in the sight of the law and the law equally holds sway over and is superior to them all. Distinction shall be made on the basis of truth and justification only. The Quran says, *Whoever does an atom's weight of good, shall see it. And whoever does an atom's weight of evil, shall see it* (Quran, 99:7-8).

In the collective form all have an equal position. The powerful support the weak and in this way the entire society serves every individual. 'The example of a Muslim in the matter of mutual love and affection is that of a body. When one of its organs is infected with a disease, all other organs suffer from fever and sleeplessness in sympathy.' (Muslim and Aḥmad)

Islam has been constantly proclaiming that humanity is a united body, and that all its individuals are the offspring of the same parents. Human society is like a tree and when the wind blows all its branches at all levels, high and low without distinction will move. It is also useful to note that the Quran addresses people in such a way that it reinforces the feeling of unity of mankind. It says in numerous places, "O mankind" or "O children of Adam." Similarly, the followers of Islam have been addressed as, "O you who believe" and "O you believers" without distinguishing one nation over the other or one group over another group.

Where the laws of Islamic Civilization are concerned, every aspect of them is based on the principle equality of people. In prayer, all people stand before Allah without there being any place of distinction for a monarch, a leader, or a scholar. In fasting too, everybody abstains from food alike and there is no distinctive facility for the leader, the rich or the noble ones. In Hajj, men wear one type of clothing, stand in one place and perform the same rites. There is no distinction between those living far and those living near, between the strong and the weak or between the nobles and common people.

If one takes a look at the civil code, one will find that all are treated on the basis of truth and justice. The main objective of legislation is the dispensation of justice. Preventing oppression is the flag that the law carries in order to protect the oppressed. Again, when one studies the criminal law, we see that all men are equally liable to punishment in case of violation of the legal limits. The murderer receives capital punishment, the thief gets punished, and whoever transgresses is disciplined. The murderer may be a scholar or an ignorant person and the murdered person may be a rich or poor person. There is no difference whether the oppressor is a leader of the believers or a weaver and the oppressed is a non-Arab or an Arab from the East or from the West, as all are the same in the eyes of the law. The Quran says, *The free for the free, the slave for the slave, and the woman for the woman* (Quran, 2:178).

Islamic Law is still more magnanimous when it establishes human dignity for all regardless of faith, race or color. The Quran declares, *We have honored the Children of Adam* (Quran, 17:70). This honor is the birthright of everyone, and with respect to creed, knowledge and the mode of living, it provides the same opportunities for all. It is the duty of the Islamic State to support them in all these matters without distinction. The *Sharīᶜah* takes man to an even higher plane when it places the basis of being rewarded and punished on their intentions and not on their outward observance. "Allah does not look at your forms but looks at your hearts." Thus, the intention is the basis of reward or punishment. "Verily all actions are but by intentions, and for everyone is what he intended." The intention which is accepted by Allah is the intention of good, of benefiting people and of seeking the pleasure of Allah without looking for material and financial benefits. The Quran says, *Worship your Lord and do good so that you may become successful* (Quran, 22:78).

When one does good to seek the pleasure of Allah, it is not

right to expect anything in return from the one benefited. The Quran says, *And because of the love of Allah they offer food to the indigent, the orphan, and the captive [saying], "We feed you for the sake of Allah alone; no reward do we desire from you, nor any thanks"* (Quran, 76:8–9).

Islamic legislation takes its philanthropy to the climax when it holds humans, animals, plants, inanimate objects, the earth and the heavens all in servitude to Allah and obedience to the laws of nature Allah created. The Quran reminds every believer in a beautiful manner in every unit of the prayer, *Praise be to Allah, Lord of the worlds, Most Gracious, Most Merciful* (Quran, 2–3).

In this way, it demands every Muslim to remember that he is part of the universe, the creation of the Most Gracious, the Most Merciful Creator, whose mercy extends to everyone and everything. Therefore, every Muslim ought to make himself the manifestation of His attribute of mercy with regards to his needs, although Allah does not in the least stand in need of his devotion and service.

These were the manifestations of the principles of philanthropy of Islamic Civilization. However, what was the reality? Did these principles remain on paper like the Charter of Human Rights of the United Nations, whose anniversary is celebrated every year whilst the powers of the world trample them underfoot every day and every hour throughout the year? Were these principles confined to the countries which proclaimed them, like the principles of the French Revolution that remained limited to the confines of France only, whilst those in the French dominions, colonies and those under mandatory rule were denied the privileges of liberty, equality and fraternity? Were any new statues erected, like the Statue of Liberty in New York, whereas in the world outside American policies often ignore liberty, freedom and peace?

History is the most truthful witness. Here, one finds the philanthropy of Islamic Civilization and the reality of its individuals' and leaders' attitudes.

Abū Dharr, an Arab from the tribe of Ghifār, became angry with Bilāl of Abyssinia, the freed slave of Abū Bakr, may Allah be pleased with him. Abū Dharr and Bilāl were both Companions of the Prophet. The dispute intensified until Abū Dharr in his fury said to Bilāl, "O son of a black woman!" Bilāl complained to the Prophet ﷺ who addressed Abū Dharr saying, "Did you call him a name reviling his mother? It appears that you still have traces of *jāhiliyyah* [ignorance] in you!" Abū Dharr thought that *jāhiliyyah* was a kind of sexual immorality or moral deviation and thus said, "At this ripe age, O Messenger of Allah?" The Prophet ﷺ said in reply, "Yes, they are your brothers." Abū Dharr regretted what he had said and repented, and out of extreme repentance and humility requested Bilāl to trample his face with his feet.

Once, during the period of the Prophet ﷺ, a woman called Fāṭimah, of the tribe of Banū Makhzūm was found guilty of theft. She was brought to the Prophet ﷺ in order to be punished. The Quraysh very much resented this since it involved their tribal prestige and dignity. So they thought of intercession by somebody for the remission of her punishment. It was therefore decided after deliberation to send Usāma ibn

Zayd for such intercession, since he was very much liked by the Prophet ﷺ. He was approached to intercede for Fāṭimah and talked to the Prophet ﷺ about this issue. The Prophet ﷺ got very angry and said to Usāma, "You have destroyed your people, because if a noble among you stole something, he would be left; whereas if a weak one amongst you stole something, he would be punished. By Allah! If it was Fāṭimah the daughter of Muḥammad who stole, I would have cut her hands."

Qays ibn Mutatiyyah, a hypocrite, once came to a gathering in which Salmān al-Fārisī, Suhayb al-Rūmī, and Bilāl al-Ḥabashī were present. He said, "Aws and Khazraj have rendered some service to this person [meaning the Prophet Muḥammad] so what have those [meaning Bilāl, Suhayb and Salmān] done to deserve this honor?" Muᶜādh ibn Jabal got up and caught him by the scruff of his neck dragged him to where the Prophet ﷺ was seated and told him what Qays had said. The Prophet became angry and dragging his sheet after him, he proceeded towards the mosque. The usual summons for the gathering of the believers in the mosque were given and the Prophet ﷺ said, "O people! Always remember that your Lord is one, and your father [Adam] is one, and your faith is also one and the same."

ᶜAdī ibn Ḥātim al-Ṭā'ī, whilst still a non-Muslim, went to Madinah one day and attended a circle of the Messenger of Allah ﷺ. Around him were his Companions who had just returned from a battle, still wearing their gear. He saw the awe in which they all sat around the Prophet ﷺ and their respect for him. Then a poor slave woman came to the Prophet and said, "I need to say something to you in secret, O Messenger of Allah!" He told her, "Find a place in the city where we can discuss it in private." He then left with her and spoke to her for a long time and then returned. When ʿAdī saw this concern for humanity, he became a Muslim.

After twenty-one years of struggle, the Prophet ﷺ conquered Makkah and those who had fought him, driven him out and denied him. Even then he called them to the same thing and kept in view those principles which he had preached bare footed in the vales of Makkah, or had enforced in Madinah as a ruler when he was laying the foundations of a new civilization in Islamic history. That day he proclaimed those principles which he had been preaching while he had not yet gained his final victory. Standing at the gate of the Kaʿbah he said, "O people of Quraysh! This day Allah has put an end to your pride of the *Jāhiliyyah* and also the pride of your ancestry. Keep in mind that all men are the offspring of Adam, and Adam was made out of clay." The Quraysh, who held an exalted position in Arabian Society and had a high opinion of themselves, listened to him in silence with bowed heads. On this occasion he recited the following Quranic verse, *O mankind! We created you from a single [pair] of a male and a female, and made you into nations and tribes so that you may know each other. Verily the most honored of you in the sight of Allah is [one who is] the most God-fearing of you* (Quran, 49:13).

When it came to the period of the Caliphate of Abū Bakr, he came forward as a ruler whose heart was full of sympathy for mankind. Notwithstanding his position as the head of the Islamic State, he came to the girls of the locality whose fathers had become martyrs in religious wars. He milked their goats for them and assured them that his new responsibilities would not stand between him and his previous routine [of such benevolent acts].

ʿUmar ibn al-Khaṭṭāb was an exemplary glorious Caliph—sympathetic to the weak, firm on truth and a Caliph who judged all as equal. He deprived himself to give to others, stayed hungry so others were fed and went door to door asking people about their living conditions.

Once he saw an old man begging in the marketplace. He asked, "Who are you, old man?" He replied, "I am an old man asking for *jizyah* and some money to live with." He was from among the Jews living in Madinah. ʿUmar said to him, "O old man! We have not done justice to you. In your youth we took *jizyah* from you and have left you to look after yourself in your old age." Holding him by the hand, he led him to his own house and prepared food for him. He then issued orders to the treasurer of the Bayt al-Māl so that the old man and all others like him would regularly be given an allowance which should suffice for them and their dependents.

ʿUmar ibn al-Khaṭṭāb was walking through a street in Madinah, when he saw a very lean young girl moving along shakily. He said, "What is this child's sad plight? Does anyone know her?" His son ʿAbdullāh said to him, "Do you not recognize her, O Amīr al-Mu'minīn?" He replied, "No." ʿAbdullāh said, "She is one your daughters!" ʿUmar asked, "And which one of my daughters is she?" ʿAbdullāh said, "She is the daughter of ʿAbdullāh the son of ʿUmar [granddaughter]." ʿUmar said,

"Why then is she in such a condition?" His son said to him, "Whatever you have, you have not given any to us." ʿUmar said in reply to his complaint, "By Allah! I have nothing for you more than I can give out to the believers in general, whether it meets your needs or not. The Book of Allah stands to decide the just amongst us."

Once a caravan came to Madinah with many women and children. ʿUmar ibn al-Khaṭṭāb said to ʿAbd al-Raḥmān ibn ʿAwf, 'Can you stand guard on them tonight?' So ʿUmar and ʿAbd al-Raḥmān ibn ʿAwf kept awake that night together and prayed *tahajjud*. ʿUmar, on hearing a baby's cry, approached the mother and said to her, "Fear Allah and look after your child carefully." Saying this, he returned to his position. Once again, he heard the child crying, and going over to her mother once again gave her the same advice. During the last part of the night the child cried once again. ʿUmar came to the mother and said, "Woe to you! You appear not to be a good mother. How is it that your child could not sleep peacefully during the night." The woman, not knowing that she was speaking to the Amīr al-Mu'minīn, said in reply, "O servant of Allah, you have pestered me several times during the night. I want to wean her forcefully [before time], but the child doesn't comply." ʿUmar asked her, "Why?" She said in reply, "Because ʿUmar grants allowances only for such children that have been weaned." ʿUmar asked, "How old is he?" She replied that he was only a few months old. Then ʿUmar asked the woman not to be hasty in weaning her child. He then led the morning prayer in such a state that his weeping made the recital of the Quran inaudible. At the end of the prayer he said, "ᶜUmar is ruined. How many Muslim children has he killed!" He then ordered someone to declare to the mothers not to hasten in weaning their children, as allowances would be given to every newborn child.

Surely the entire history of mankind is unable to boast of such a brilliant and glorious incident. No other civilization in the world can present a person like ᶜUmar. He kept awake the whole night, keeping guard over the caravan as the caravan slept in peace. One should bear in mind that he was the head of the Islamic State and wielded great authority and power that had defeated the then super powers of Rome and Persia. In spite of all that, he did what a petty guard detailed to patrol the vicinity of a caravan in its sojourn would not even do. He drew the attention of the crying child's mother to her baby and asked her to keep it quiet. Who is there among the greatest personalities of the history of mankind that comes close to the great human concern of ᶜUmar?

Islamic Civilization has more glorious incidents to present. ᶜUmar's servant, Aslam, relates, "I went out with ᶜUmar one night into the open area outside Madinah. We were out on a fact-finding mission to distant hamlets on the outskirts of Madinah. From a distance we observed a glow far off. ᶜUmar said, 'I believe the darkness of the night and the cold have compelled some horsemen to sojourn there. Let us go and see.' We proceeded at a brisk pace and reached that spot. We saw a woman sitting there with some children around her crying. ᶜUmar greeted her and asked, 'What is wrong?' The woman said in reply, 'They are hungry.' Then ᶜUmar asked her, 'What is in the fire?' The woman said, 'Only water to console the children so that they may remain quiet and go to sleep.' What the woman wanted to convey was that ʿUmar was not fair and just to them. ʿUmar said to her, 'My good woman! What does ʿUmar know about your state of affairs?' To which she replied, 'Why then should he hold the high office of Caliph when he is unaware of our condition?' ʿUmar then said to me, 'Let us go now.' We left from there in a rush and reached the House of Flour and ʿUmar took a bag of flour and a container of oil and asked me to load the bag on his back. I offered my services but he angrily brushed aside my offer saying, 'Can you relieve me of my burden on the Day of Reckoning too?' So I loaded the bag on his back, and then we hastened towards our destination at a fast enough pace. Soon he placed the bag and, taking out some flour from it, gave it to the woman and asked her to knead it while he himself offered to fan the fire to a flame. So he started blowing the fire below the pot. His beard was thick and I saw smoke percolating through his beard. He went on blowing at it until the food was ready, and he asked the woman to bring some vessel. When she brought a platter he poured out the contents of the pot into it and asked the woman to feed the children while he himself fanned to cool it. We sat there until all of them had eaten to their fill. What was left of the flour and oil was handed over to her and then ʿUmar got up and I followed suit. The woman said, 'Allah bless you. You are more deserving of that high office than the Amīr al-Mu'minīn.' ʿUmar said to her, 'When tomorrow you come to see the Amīr al-Mu'minīn, you will find me there, Allah willing.' After that ʿUmar left and then retraced his steps and hid himself close to where they were staying. I said to him that it was not proper on his part to observe them from the place of his concealment. He kept quiet. We saw that the children were playing merrily and then they went to sleep. ʿUmar thanked Allah and got up and, turning to me, said, 'Aslam! Hunger was growing in their stomachs, keeping them awake and making them cry. I would not have been at ease until I had seen what you have seen.'"

One of the unique incidents relating to sympathy and equality in the history of mankind is another story involving ʿUmar. It was usual for him to go out during the nights to see the conditions with which people lived. One night he found himself in one of the many valleys of Madinah. All of a sudden, he heard somebody crying in a nearby tent, at whose door was standing a man. ʿUmar greeted him in the proper manner and asked him who he was. He said that he was a Bedouin who had come to Madinah to ask the Amīr al-Mu'minīn for help. Then ʿUmar asked him about the crying and wailing inside the tent, a question the Bedouin tried to evade, saying that since it did not concern him, he should not interest himself in it and be on his way. Little did he know he was talking to the Amīr al-Mu'minīn. However, on the insistence of ʿUmar, he told him that his wife was in labor and had no one to help her with the delivery. ʿUmar went back home and asked his wife, Umm Kulthūm bint ʿAlī and said, "Shall I facilitate a reward for you from Allah?" She asked, "What is it?" He informed her of the situation and told her to take clothes for the newborn baby and whatever the woman would require including food. ʿUmar took all those things from her and started to walk with Umm Kulthūm following him. They reached the house and ʿUmar said to his wife, "Go to the woman." He sat down with the man, lit the fire and began to cook whatever they had brought. All this time, the man did not know with whom he was sitting. Meanwhile, the woman in the tent gave birth and Umm Kulthūm called out from the house, "O Amīr al-Mu'minīn, give good news of a baby boy to your friend." When the Bedouin heard her, he was awe-struck and began moving away from ʿUmar. However, ʿUmar reassured him and said, "Stay where you are." He then carried the cooking pot and asked his wife to feed the woman. When she had eaten, he offered food to the man saying, "Eat it, you have stayed up the whole night." Umm Kulthūm then came out and ʿUmar said to the man, "Come to me tomorrow and I shall see to it that your needs are provided for." When he came to him the next morning, ʿUmar granted an allowance for his new born baby and was himself given help.

I cannot recall from all the biographies I have read of great figures, an incident more glorious, outstanding and sublime sentiments of fraternity than the one cited above. There is an incident with George Washington, where he was once walking along the road and saw that some soldiers were trying to lift a stone but were unable to do so. Their supervisor was standing close by but not lending a helping hand. George Washington asked him to assist them, but he refused saying that it was below his dignity. Washington put his cloak on the road and helped them to lift the boulder, saying to them, "Whenever you need any help of this kind, then ask the House of Washington."

Certainly, this is an exceptional incident and is an example of a high standard of morality. However, it does not compare with the incident of ʿUmar cited above. ʿUmar, sacrificing his sleep and comfort came out in order to find out about the people's condition. He found a woman in labor who had no one to help her, so he came home, loaded himself with provisions, and he and his wife went to attend to the needs of the mother and the new born infant in a Bedouin tent far away from where they were living. The wife of the Caliph played the role of a maid-servant, a midwife, and the Caliph himself took upon the role of the cook. Is there a single example of this loftiness in man's psyche? This is one of those brilliant incidents that make ʿUmar so great, and it is also one of the dazzling aspects of Islamic Civilization that it moulded a simple Arab like ʿUmar into a persona that even today occupies the highest stand among the great men in the history of mankind, just as Islamic Civilization stands out among the other civilizations of the world.

ʿUmar is not an isolated example presented as a perfect and affectionate person of Islamic Civilization. There are many others. The lives of Abū Bakr, ʿUthmān and ʿAlī, may Allah be pleased with them all, were also moulded in the mould of perfect humanity, regarding mercy and affection. Also the lives of ʿUmar ibn ʿAbd al-ʿAzīz, Ṣalāḥuddīn al-Ayyūbī and many other great personalities, the scholars, the jurists, the philosophers and the leaders also present countless immortal examples as evidence in favor of the glorious Islamic Civilization from every aspect.

CHAPTER FOUR

RACIAL EQUALITY

ANOTHER ASPECT OF the philanthropy of the Islamic Civilization is that it strengthened the basis of real equality irrespective of color and race. So after the proclamation of the Quran, *Verily the most honored of you in the sight of Allah is [one who is] the most god-fearing of you* (Quran, 49:13), the Messenger of Allah ﷺ said in his last sermon on the occasion of Hajj before his departure from this world, "All men are from Adam, and Adam is from clay. There is no superiority of an Arab over a non-Arab, nor a white person over a black person except in *taqwā* [level of piety and God-Consciousness]."

This equality did not stop at the level of principles advocated in formal occasions, as is the case with the contemporary civilization; rather it was equality that was implemented and executed as a normal routine without causing any special attention. Thus this equality was implemented in the mosques where white and black would meet on one platform and stand in humility and devotion in the worship of Allah, the Exalted. The white man did not take any offence at the black man standing next to him, and there was no superiority of white over black. This equality was implemented in the Hajj where different elements of humanity would meet. The Messenger of Allah ﷺ ordered Bilāl, the Abyssinian, on the day of the conquest of Makkah, to ascend the Kaʿbah and make the *adhān* and to proclaim the Word of Truth. The Kaʿbah was a place of divine sanctuary even with the Arabs of *Jāhiliyyah,* and it is the magnificent direction of prayer in Islam Thus, how does a black slave like Bilāl ascend on it and have the Kaʿbah under his feet? Although incidents similar to this cannot be imagined in contemporary civilization, the Islamic Civilization accomplished this fourteen hundred years ago. The ascension of Bilāl onto the roof of the Kaʿbah was nothing but the declaration of human dignity over all things and that a man deserves this honor because of his knowledge, his intellect, his character, his faith and not because of his body or color. Therefore, the color of a person cannot advance him if his record of deeds draws him back.

Thus, the Messenger of Allah ﷺ was not pleased with Abū Dharr, notwithstanding his position as one of the high ranking Companions of the Prophet, when he insulted Bilāl saying, "O son of a black woman!" The Messenger of Allah did not tolerate this, rather he reprimanded him and said, "You still have traces of *jāhiliyyah* in you." This is the point which marks the line of demarcation between knowledge and ignorance. In other words it demarcates the real human civilization and the civilization of the *jāhiliyyah.*

The civilization that does not make one race superior over another, nor one color over another is the civilization that the noble and intelligent human builds, and thus conscious noble humanity is pleased. The civilization which gives superiority to whites and degrades the black so that only the whites are happy and the colored are in misery takes humanity back to the blind and dark ages. "You have traces of *jāhiliyyah* in you" is a description of the *jāhilī* civilization which calls for racial discrimination and this is what Islamic Civilization has fought in all fields of life—in the mosque, in the school, in the court, in the leadership and with friends and foe alike.

When Muslims conquered Egypt and advanced to the Fort of Bablion, Muqauqis the ruler of Egypt sent a delegation to speak to Muslims to find out what they wanted. He also expressed a desire to receive a delegation of Muslims. Therefore, ʿAmr ibn al-ʿĀṣ sent a delegation comprising ten people. This delegation was led by ʿUbāda ibn Samit, and he alone was authorized to talk to Muqauqis. ʿUbāda was tall and very black, and when this delegation approached Muqauqis to speak to him, he was struck by his appearance alone, and he said to the members of the delegation, "Keep this black person away from me, and bring forward somebody else to speak to me." The members of the delegation unanimously said to him, "He is superior to us in intellect, knowledge, opinion, insight and in every other way. He is our leader. We all turn to him for his opinion and advice. Moreover, our governor has given him some particular instructions, and has ordered us not to go against him in any matter whatsoever." At this, Muqauqis said to the delegation, "How could you agree to make him your leader and superior, whereas he ought to have been your subordinate?" To this the delegation replied, "No, despite the fact you see him as black, he is the best among us in knowledge, in nobility, in intellect and opinion, and we do not look down upon the black man." Muqauqis said to ʿUbāda, "Come forward, O black [man] and speak to me gently for I fear your color, and if you were to talk to me in a harsh tone, my distress shall be all the greater." ʿUbāda, noticing Muqauqis' fear of black people, said, "We have in our army a thousand people darker than me."

How bright and sublime the humanity of Islamic Civilization was! The "civilized" people of the twentieth century see the black person as intellectually inferior. They do not see blacks as fit to being counted equally among the whites, who ask, "How can they be advanced in knowledge and opinion?" Islamic Civilization put an end to all these false notions and showed the stupidity of such norms. It gives preference to the black over the white if the black man is superior in terms of knowledge, opinion and courage. ʿUbāda ibn Samit was not the only black man that Islamic Civilization elevated to the position of leadership.

ʿAbd al-Mālik ibn Marwān used to order someone to declare, at the start of season of Hajj, that none should be allowed to give legal opinions except ʿAṭā ibn Abī Ribāḥ—the leader, scholar and jurist of Makkah. Does one know what ʿAṭā looked like? He was black, one-eyed, flat-nosed, lame and curly haired. When he was sitting in front of his students it appeared as if a black bird was sitting in a field of cotton. However, it was this person whom the Islamic Civilization made a leader and a person to whom people turned for legal opinions. He was a school of thought in his own right and thousands of students (of all races and hues) graduated from his school. His students upheld him in honor, love and respect.

In Islamic Civilization there have been several scholars of African origin and this did not prevent them from making headway in the field of knowledge and literature. It did not prevent them from becoming men of letters associating with Caliphs as poets, or jurists writing books that were considered to be references in Islamic Law. Examples are ʿUthmān ibn ʿAlī al-Zaylaʿī, who wrote a commentary on *Kanz al-Ḍaqā'iq*, a book of Ḥanafī jurisprudence, and al-Ḥāfiẓ Jamāluddīn Abī Muḥammad ʿAbdullāh ibn Yūsuf al-Zaylaʿī (d. 762) who wrote *Nasab al-Rayah*. Both of them were African and, specifically, from Zayla in Abyssinia. Kafur al-Akhshidi is also a well-known person. He was a dark-skinned freed slave who ruled Egypt in the fourth Islamic century and whose name has been immortalized by the famous poet Mutanabbī through his eulogy.

In short, the Islamic Civilization never discriminated between black and white, nor was there ever any colony established for black people, which totally segregated them from the whites. Nor were the rights of black people curtailed so as to give white people the upper hand. Rather, Islamic Civilization was a real human civilization which valued humanity. It looked upon all men under the norm of the truth and good and did not see whiteness and blackness, only deeds and actions. The Quran says, *Whoever does an atom's weight of good, shall see it. And whoever does an atom's weight of evil, shall see it* (Quran, 99:7-8).

It is correct that during the past fifty years, discrimination between people on the basis of color has been recognized as absurd and that discriminating between blacks and whites came to be seen as a barbaric act. It is also well known that Islamic Civilization would not tolerate such discrimination and that it was the most famous civilization known to spread fraternity and equality between people. It is a tragedy that in this era of progress, and in spite of the formation of the United Nations and the proclamation of the Charter of Human Rights, one still witnesses racial discrimination in South Africa, the fearful tyrannies of colonialism in Kenya and the situation of the African Americans and the colored people of the United States. It is more amazing to see that those who are upholding apartheid in South Africa, those who are oppressing the blacks politically and economically in Kenya and those who make life terrible for the African Americans are not from the East and cannot be accused of conservatism, backwardness and foolishness. They are all the sons of the civilised and developed nations of the West, and are regarded as the outstanding members of the United Nations. These so-called sons of civilization of Europe never tire of ridiculing the men of the East for backwardness, conservatism and prejudice, but what they themselves are doing is not hidden from public view. The governments guilty of these crimes are those that are regarded as important observers of the United Nations.

The government of South Africa, for example, had long adopted the policy of apartheid, and apportioned separate rights and obligations for black and white, notwithstanding the constant protest and strong opposition. One of the strange land laws of that country was that the ruler had the authority to allot land to whomever he wished on a 999 year-lease; and if the size of the land did not exceed 5,000 acres, the ruler had the power to allot that piece of land. By 1925, this had resulted in the Boers having on average 5,000 acres of land per head and the native people having eight acres of land per head. Moreover, to keep the blacks and the whites segregated, totally separate residential areas were set aside for the black population; they were then unable to visit the spacious spreads of the white men. When the latter stood in dire need of very cheap labor they took the black people into their employ, but as soon as the work was over, they were forced to return from the fields of the whites to the squalor.

When one analyzes the situation of the African Americans one observes the appalling conditions of oppression. [At one time] one found that in about twenty states of the U.S.A., the black population was barred from receiving education with white people in the same school or college. Moreover, a black person was unable to sit at the same table as a white person or enter or leave through the same doors that the white men used. A black person was forbidden to sit next to a white person on a bus or train. Most incredible of all was an announcement made by an officer in charge of the burial ground for dogs in Washington in 1947—he said that he would not allow the dogs of black men to be buried in the graveyard where the dogs of the white men were buried.

The famous American economist Victor Barlow once said, "The venom of racial discrimination has spread the length and breadth of the country, and has seeped into American life to such an extent that the common people have now become used to the fact that no opportunity should be lost in debasing and humiliating the African Americans and other minorities."

In Colombia City in 1846, an African American man and his mother went to a repair shop to get their radio mended. After they had paid the shopkeeper the repair charges, they found that the defect in their radio persisted and had not been repaired properly. The mother said to the shopkeeper, 'I paid you thirteen dollars and the radio still doesn't work.' The shopkeeper ordered his assistant to throw her out of the shop. The assistant kicked the poor woman and she fell on her face. This enraged her son who beat the assistant and floored him. A white neighbor, witnessing this began to cry that the miscreant must be put to death. A crowd soon gathered that was insistent on revenge. Eventually, the boy was rescued from the crowd and put into prison. But the crowd was not satisfied. They rushed to the African American neighborhood to avenge themselves on some black women and their sons. The police cordoned off this quarter of the town and did not let the inhabitants run to safety, with the result that the enraged crowd fell to ravage, destruction and arson. The houses were set on fire and the inhabitants shot at, leaving many dead and wounded.

Let one compare the above incident with an incident which took place [fourteen] hundred years ago. A black girl named Fartuna wrote a letter to the Caliph ʿUmar ibn ʿAbd al-ʿAzīz that the boundary wall of her house was very low and that poachers scaled the wall and stole her hens. ʿUmar ibn ʿAbd al-ʿAzīz wrote back to her saying that the governor of Egypt had been ordered to have the wall of her house raised and to undertake other necessary repairs to the house also. He wrote to the governor of Egypt Ayyūb ibn Sharḥabīl, "Fartuna the freed slave girl has written to me complaining that the boundary wall of her house is so low that thieves enter at night and steal her hens. She wants it to be raised and reinforced. When you receive this letter go to her house and in your own presence have the wall raised and properly strengthened." When Ayyūb ibn Sharḥabīl received the letter he went out in search of Fartuna and found her to be a poor black woman. He informed her of what the Amīr al-Mu'minīn had written and he himself raised and strengthened the wall.

CHAPTER FIVE

RELIGIOUS TOLERANCE

RELIGIOUS TOLERANCE IS a new aspect of the humanitarianism of the unique Islamic Civilization. It is something new to the history of belief and religion, new to the ancient civilizations developed by a specific religion or a specific nation. When Islam laid the foundations of a new civilization, it did not adopt a narrow-minded approach to the religions of the past. It also did not adopt a fanatical attitude to the opinions of various schools of thought. Rather, it took as its motto the Quranic verses, *So announce the glad tidings to My servants, those who listen to the words and follow the best of it* (Quran, 39:17-18).

The principles of religious tolerance in Islamic Civilization are as follows: All revealed religions have sprung from the same fountain. The Quran says, *The same religion He has established for you is as that which He enjoined on Nūḥ—and what We now reveal to you—and enjoined on Ibrāhīm, Mūsā, ʿĪsā, saying, "Establish the religion and do not become divided therein"* (Quran, 42:13).

The prophets are a brotherhood and there is no superiority of one over the other from the viewpoint of the *risāla*. Thus it is binding on Muslims to believe in all the Prophets of Allah. The

Quran says, *Say, "We believe in Allah and in that which He has revealed to us and to Ibrāhīm, Ismāʿīl, Isḥāq, Yaʿqūb, al-ʿAsbāṭ and that which was revealed to Mūsā, ʿĪsā and that which was revealed to the prophets from their Lord, We make no difference between one and another and we bow in submission to Him* (Quran, 2:136).

There is no compulsion in religion. Rather, it has been left to the inclination and pleasure of people, *Let there be no compulsion in religion* (Quran, 2:256). *Will you then compel mankind, against their will, to believe?* (Quran, 10:33).

The places of worship of all divine religions are respectable places and protecting them is just as essential as protecting the mosques of Muslims, *For had it not been for Allah's checking some men by means of others, monasteries, churches, synagogues, and mosques, wherein the name of Allah is often mentioned, would have been destroyed* (Quran, 22:40).

It is not permitted for people to kill one another or oppress one another on the grounds of the difference of creed. Rather, they should cooperate with one another in promoting the cause of good and in eradicating evil. The Quran says, *Help one another in benevolence and piety, and help not one another in sin and transgression* (Quran, 5:2). As for the differences that have appeared between them, Allah Himself will judge between them on the Day of Judgment, *The Jews said the Christians were misguided; and the Christians said it was the Jews who were misguided; although both are readers of the Book [the Torah and Gospel]. Those who know nothing said the same. Allah will judge between them on the Day of Resurrection concerning that wherein they differ* (Quran, 2:113).

The disparity between people in this life and with Allah will be judged according to what good and piety one has done for one's own self and for others. The Messenger of Allah ﷺ said, "The people are like the children of Allah and the most beloved to Him is the one who is most beneficial to His children." (Al-Bazzār). The Quran also says, *Verily, the most honored of you in the sight of Allah is [one who is] the most God-fearing of you* (Quran, 49:13).

Difference of creed should not become an obstacle in doing good or enjoining the good treatment of blood relations and respecting guests. The Quran says, *This day [all] good things are made lawful for you. The food of those who have received the Book is lawful for you, and your food is lawful for them. And so are the virtuous women of the believers, and the virtuous women of those who received the Book before you [are lawful for you]* (Quran, 5:5).

Despite the difference in the creeds of the people, they have the right to debate with one another in ways that are best and with the best of manners. Convincing evidence should be put forward. The Quran says, *And do not dispute with the People of the Book except in the best of ways* (Quran, 29:46). Islam does not permit rudeness with opponents nor does it allow one to curse their beliefs even if they are polytheists. The Quran says, *Revile not those whom they pray to apart from Allah, lest they wrongfully revile Allah through ignorance* (Quran, 6:108).

However, when the Muslim *Ummah* is being oppressed because of its creed and ideology, it becomes incumbent to combat the enemy and put an end to the mischief. The Quran says, *And fight them until sedition and persecution are no more and religion is all Allah's* (Quran, 2:193). *Allah only forbids you to make allies with those who have fought against you on account of your religion and driven you from your homes or abetted others to do so* (Quran, 60:9).

Once the Muslim *Ummah* has become victorious over those who fight them in the matter of the faith of the *Ummah* or its freedom, they are not permitted to take revenge upon the vanquished people. It would suffice that the conquered people submit to the Islamic State and sincerely stick to their covenant so that they may come to have the position: "They have the same rights as we have, and [they] have the same obligations that we have."

These are the principles of religious tolerance in Islam upon which Islamic Civilization was built. These principles make it obligatory for every Muslim to believe in all the Prophets of Allah and speak about them with due respect. Muslims should also not oppress the followers of any of the Prophets; rather they should deal with them fairly and treat them gently and kindly. Neighbors are to be treated kindly and their invitations should also be accepted. A Muslim man can marry a woman of the People of the Book so that family relations may be created and blood ties may be established. Islam has made it incumbent on the Islamic State to protect their places of worship, not to interfere in their creed and be just in cases involving them. In the matter of rights and obligations, they are to be treated as Muslims, and their honor, life and future are protected just as the honor of the life and future of Muslims are protected.

Such are the bases upon which Islamic Civilization is built, and the world witnessed for the first time a religion that created a civilization without a shade of prejudice against other religions. It was a civilization which did not prevent non-Muslims from being involved in the social arena of life. This tolerance continued to be the norm of the Islamic Civilization from the day that Prophet Muḥammad ﷺ laid its foundations. However, when Islamic Civilization entered the days of decay, these principles were lost, injunctions were forgotten, the people became ignorant of their religion and thus they were far removed from this noble religious tolerance.

When the Messenger of Allah ﷺ migrated to Madinah, it had a large Jewish population. The first thing he did at a government level was to negotiate a covenant between the Muslims and the Jews, by which it became binding that the Islamic State respect the beliefs of the Jews and protect them from harm of any kind whatsoever. On the other side, the Jews pledged to stand by the Muslims in case of an attack on Madinah. Through this treaty the Prophet ﷺ inculcated the principles and elements of religious tolerance in the conscience of Islamic Civilization from the first day of its inception.

The Messenger of Allah had Jewish and Christian neighbors and he would always treat them kindly and benevolently, sending gifts to them and accepting gifts from them. Taking advantage of this attitude of the Prophet, a Jewish woman one day sent a roasted leg of mutton after it had been injected with a lethal poison. She could do this since she was sure that the Prophet ﷺ would accept gifts from her as he was on good neighborly terms with her. When the Abyssinian Christians came to Madinah, the Messenger of Allah made arrangements for them to stay in the mosque, and took upon himself the responsibilities of hospitality and service. He also said, "These people respected and treated our Companions with honor and thus I wish to host them myself."

Once a delegation of Christians from Najrān came to Madinah. They too were brought to the mosque to stay, and were allowed to conduct their service in the mosque in their own way. Thus they would be praying in one part of the mosque and the Messenger of Allah and his Companions would be praying in another part. When these people presented their own faith putting forth arguments in its support the Prophet ﷺ listened to them attentively and very gently, with due respect and courtesy, replied to their religious assertions. The Prophet accepted the gift sent by Muqauqis, the ruler of Egypt, and by the slave girl, who had the honor of giving birth to the Prophet's son Ibrāhīm, who lived only a few months. He further advised the Muslims, "You should remain well-wishers of the Copts since you have relatives among them."

After the Prophet ﷺ, the Caliphs ruled on the same lines and maintained his high-ranking, humanitarian policy of religious tolerance. Thus, we find that when ʿUmar, the second rightly guided Caliph, entered Bayt al-Maqdis as a conqueror, he accepted the condition laid down by the Christians of Palestine that no Jew should be allowed to settle there. While he was in the great church of Bayt al-Maqdis, the time of ʿAṣr Prayer approached. However, he abstained from praying in the church, lest Muslims in times to come claim it as a mosque on the basis that ʿUmar had prayed there.

Once a woman from Egypt lodged a complaint with ʿUmar that ʿAmr ibn al-ʿĀṣ had annexed her house for the extension of the mosque against her will. ʿUmar asked ʿAmr ibn al-ʿĀṣ for an explanation. He explained that the number of the believers coming to the mosque for prayer far exceeded the capacity of the mosque. The house of the complainant was adjacent to the mosque and she was offered the price of her property and far in excess of its real worth, but she declined the offer. Therefore, in view of public interest, it was demolished to form part of the mosque, and the costs were deposited in the Bayt al-Māl, so that she might take it whenever she pleased. Apparently the explanation offered by ʿAmr ibn al-ʿĀṣ was reasonable, and our present day law also permits it. However, to ʿUmar it was not acceptable and he ordered the demolition of the portion of the mosque built on the site of the woman's house and ordered the re-construction of her house as it had been before.

This is the nature of tolerance which dominated every society influenced by the principles of Islamic Civilization. Thus one comes across many manifestations of religious tolerance unparalleled in the history of mankind and even in any civilization of the present era. In the unique Islamic Civilization, it has been seen time and again that the mosque and the church were standing side by side. The religious leaders of the churches had full powers in the religious affairs of their co-religionists and their churches, and the Islamic State never interfered in these matters. Rather, it often happened that they themselves oppressed one another due to their religious differences and so the Islamic State would thus mediate and justly decided their disputes. For example, the Malachi sect of the Greek Christians during the period of the Roman Empire always oppressed the Coptic Christians of Egypt. The people belonging to this sect plundered the churches of the Egyptian Copts. When Muslims conquered Egypt they returned all their properties to the Copts and meted out justice to them. Later, the Egyptian Copts avenged the excesses and tyrannies of Malachi Christians perpetrated before the advent of the Muslim rule there. Thus the Malachis lodged a complaint with the ʿAbbāsid Caliph, Hārūn al-Rashīd, who had all the properties and churches restored to the Malachis after taking them away from the Copts.

Under Islamic rule, the Christians had full freedom to perform their religious ceremonies, and their religious leaders had full authority over their co-religionists and the government never interfered in their personal affairs. The Christians themselves realized that there was such perfect freedom under the Islamic State. In this connection the name of Sultan Muḥammad, the conqueror of Constantinople, shall ever remain fresh in the history of religious tolerance. When he conquered Constantinople, it was exclusively populated by Christians and was the capital of the patriarch for the Eastern Catholic Christians. The Sultan granted amnesty to the entire Christian population and guaranteed safety of their lives, properties, their creed, their churches and their crosses. They were exempted from military service and their leaders were authorized to judge and decide all those cases that came to them from their co-religionists. The Islamic government never interfered with regards to this legislation. The Christians of Constantinople themselves felt that there was a world of difference between the attitude and behavior of Sultan Muḥammad and the Byzantine rulers of the past. The Byzantine rulers interfered in the religious differences of people and meted out preferential treatment to the followers of their own church in comparison to those of the other churches. So the Christians liked the new system of government very much and were pleased with the religious tolerance which had no parallel in their own governments. The Roman patriarch had been allowed so much authority that his position made it a case of a state within the state. For five hundred years they lived in this free atmosphere, and their freedom was so well protected that they needed no army, nor had they to pay any taxes for such security. However, it was disgraceful how the Christians took undue advantage of the special privileges allowed to them due to religious tolerance. At the close of the nineteenth and the beginning of the twentieth century, they resorted to perfidious and treacherous moves to put an end to the local authority and dominion of these towns and cities where they had lived for centuries.

A manifestation of the religious tolerance of Islamic Civilization was that when Muslims conquered the Christian lands, in many of their churches Muslims and Christians offered prayers under the same roof. The Prophet ﷺ himself in his lifetime offered the Christian delegation from Najrān the facility of praying in one section of the mosque in their own way. Similarly, after the Islamic conquest, in the Cathedral of St. John in Damascus, which later came to be called the Umayyad Mosque, Muslims did not prevent the Christians from performing their Prayers. Rather, they open heartedly allowed the Christians to pray there. The Christians willingly surrendered half of it to Muslims, who prayed there side by side with the Christians, and thus one would see Muslims and the Christians praying under the same roof, the former facing their *Qiblah* and the latter facing the East. It was a novel phenomenon which has a unique position in history, and speaks volumes about Islamic Civilization being free from religious prejudice and shows how it had been replete with religious tolerance.

Another proof of the religious tolerance of the Islamic State is that they selected the most capable people and entrusted important posts to them irrespective of their beliefs. Thus during the period of the Umayyids and ᶜAbbāsids, Christian physicians were appointed to highly responsible posts, and they were held in high esteem by the Caliphs themselves. In Baghdad and Damascus the Christian physicians were in charge of many of the medical schools for a long time. Ibn Athal, a Christian doctor, was the personal physician of Muᶜāwiyyah, and another Christian by the name of Sergeon was his scribe. Marwān had appointed Athanaseus with another Christian, Isaac, to hold important posts in Egypt, and later they were promoted to the high post of the Treasury office. Athanaseus was a man of high status who was also extremely rich. He had four thousand slaves and he owned several villages and gardens. He had a church built in al-Raha, out of the rent of the four hundred shops that he owned. His reputation as a learned person attained such a position that ᶜAbd al-Mālik, the Umayyid Caliph entrusted to his care the education and training of his younger brother, ᶜAbd al-ʿAzīz, who later became the governor of Egypt. His son was the renowned Caliph ʿUmar ibn ʿAbd al-ʿAzīz.

Among the famous Christian physicians who were honored with high-ranking jobs there was George, son of Bachtesu. He was in great favor at the court of Caliph Manṣūr, who held him in great esteem and had provided everything for his comfort and ease. George had an old wife and thus Manṣūr sent him three slave girls, which he declined saying, "My faith does not permit me marrying other women whilst my wife is still alive." Manṣūr was much pleased to hear this and raised his rank higher. When George fell ill, Manṣūr called him to Dār al-Ḍiyāfa [Guest House] and came to see him in person. George sought permission to return to his native land so that he may be buried by the side of his ancestors. Manṣūr asked him to embrace Islam so that he may enter Paradise. He refused and said, "I would like to be in the company of my ancestors whether they live in Paradise or Hell." Manṣūr laughed at this joke of his and ordered preparations for his journey home with a gift of ten thousand gold pieces.

Similarly, another Christian, Salmavaih son of Banan was the personal physician of Muʿtaṣim. When he died, Muʿtaṣim was very much grieved, wept bitterly over his loss and ordered that he should be buried in the royal fashion according to the ceremonies of his own religion. Bachtesu son of Gabriel, another Christian, was the personal physician of Mutawakkil and held a high position in his court. This person rivalled the Caliph himself in the abundance of riches, magnificent dresses and pomp and glory.

Closeness to the rulers and conferring of honor by them was more or less the same with the literati and the poets. The poets and literati were honored at the courts of Banū Ummayya and Banū ʿAbbās without any discrimination, the only condition being excellence and expertise. Everyone knows what position Akhtal held at the Umayyad court. He had the permission of the Caliph to approach him any time he pleased and would come to see the Caliph ʿAbd al-Mālik any time of the day or the night. Sometimes he was seen entering dressed in a silken gown and a cross, suspended by a golden chain from his neck and droplets of wine dropping from his beard. He is the same person who had reviled the Anṣār of Madinah in which he had said, "Disgrace and reproach lie beneath the turbans of Anṣār." At this the Anṣār were very much grieved, and they sent one of their elderly men, Nuʿmān ibn Bishir, who had the honor of being a Companion of the Prophet, to ʿAbd al-Mālik. He saw ʿAbd al-Mālik and, taking off his turban, showed its interior and his own scalp to him, saying, "Where is disgrace and reproach here?" ʿAbd al-Mālik himself apologized for this insult and pacified him with earnest supplication, but did not call Akhtal to account for his arrogance and insolence.

Besides the Caliphs, the general people of society were open-minded and their selection of friends was not restricted to followers of a particular religion. Ibrāhīm ibn Hilāl, who belonged to a particular sect of Magians, was appointed to a high position in the government and welcomed and valued poets very much. Yet his social circle was not limited to his co-religionists. Rather, he was on such good terms with the Muslim learned men and men of letters that on his death, Sharīf Radhī wrote a long poem known as *Qaṣīdah Waliyah* praising in it Ibrāhīm ibn Hilāl. It is well known that Sharīf Radhī was the leader of Hashimites and head of the Shiite community. He says in his *Qaṣīdah*:

> Did you notice whom they took away on planks?
> And did you see how the fire was extinguished.
> I did not know before your burial,
> That mountains could also be buried in graves.

Sharīf Radhī kept remembering him even after that and wrote eulogy on special occasions. Once he passed by his grave and burst into tears:

> I say to the wayfarers passing this way to come to this [grave]
> So that I may show you a seclusion-loving branch of greatness and eminence
> I mourned your loss to lighten the burden of my grieved heart, but the pain increased.
> The eulogies do not lessen the grief of calamities
> I know it is not gainful to mourn your loss.
> But the longings have made me all the more aspirant.

Under the patronage of the Caliphs, the academic circles always attracted men of learning of various creeds. Ma'mūn al-Rashīd had an academic circle of his own in which men of learning of many creeds used to meet. He used to say to them, "Keep your discourses and discussions limited to learning and the arts, and do not bring forth evidence from your religious books." By adhering to this advice sectarian problems were avoided.

The same is true of general national academic circles. Khalaf ibn al-Muthanna says, "We witnessed the meeting of an academic circle in Basra comprising of ten people. Each was unique and an expert in his own branch of learning and there were none comparable to them on the face of the earth." The ten people were Khalīl ibn Aḥmad, the well-known grammarian (Sunni); Ḥumayrī, a poet (Shiite); Sāliḥ ibn ʿAbd al-Quddusān (Atheist); Sufyān ibn Majamī (Ṣafwī sect of the Kharijites); Bashshār ibn Burd (Shawbī sect); Ḥammād Ajrad (Atheistic Nationalist); Ibn Rās Jālūt, the well known poet (Jew); Ibn Naẓīr, a philosopher (Christian); ʿUmar ibn al-Mu'ayyid (Magian); and Ibn Sanan al-Ḥarrānī, a poet (Sabian).

These people used to sit together to discuss various problems and historical events and to recite poems. It was such a friendly atmosphere that nobody could suspect that they belonged to conflicting creeds.

This religious tolerance was common in families and homes also. Often, it was witnessed that out of four brothers living in the same house, one professed the Sunni Creed, another was Shiite, a third was a Muʿtazilī and the fourth was Kharijite. All four were living in a spirit of perfect unity, love and concord.

Similarly, the situation was also witnessed that out of the two brothers living in same house, one remained occupied with his devotional acts and the other in his ludicrous fun and frolic. In this connection, a very interesting event has been narrated in books of literature. Two brothers lived together in the same house, one very pious, living on the ground floor, and the other, an impious transgressor living on the first floor. Once, some equally impious friends of the impious transgressor gathered together at his place and made a lot of noise with their songs and music. They kept it up so long that the pious brother of this transgressor could not sleep the whole night. So he came out of his apartment and called out to his brother saying, *Do then those who devise evil (plots) feel secure that Allah will not cause the earth to swallow them up* (Quran, 16:45). To which his brother replied, *But Allah will not punish them whilst you are amongst them* (Quran, 8:33).

Similarly, on the occasion of the festivals of other religions and sects, Muslims participated with great enthusiasm. Since the Umayyad dynasty, the Christians held their religious ceremonies beside the public thoroughfares and went in processions on public roads. In these processions, some people bearing crosses led the procession; and their religious leaders, in their special dress, accompanied them. Once the patriarch, Michael, entered Alexandria at the head of a magnificent procession. The front line was occupied by crosses, torches and Gospels, and the priests were raising the slogan, "God has sent us a saviour, a pastor who is the modern St. Mark." This incident relates to the period of Hishām ibn ᶜAbd al-Mālik.

During the period of Rashīd, the Christians on the occasion of Easter came out in the form of a huge procession holding aloft big crosses on pedestals. Al-Maqdisī mentions in his book *Aḥsan al-Taqasim* that on the occasion of the Christian festivals the markets of Shiraz were decorated. When the Nile flooded and the Christians celebrated their festivals of the cross, the Egyptians also participated in the celebrations.

Maqrizi writes in his book *Khitatah* that during the period of Akhshidīs, the common people made great rejoicing on the occasion of the festival of Baptism. In 330 AH, this festival was celebrated with great magnificence. Muḥammad ibn Tugaj al-Akhshidī's palace on the island of Manil was decorated with one thousand chandeliers, and the nation also followed suit with countless torches, candles and chandeliers being lighted. Thousands of Muslims and Christians gathered round water tanks and reservoirs, and the rooftops and the banks of the canals were packed to their full capacity. People put on their best dresses, and food was brought in silver and gold vessels. The night gates were not closed and most people bathed and dived in tanks under the impression that bathing on the night of the festival of Baptism was beneficial in the remedy of countless maladies.

It is amazing to note that these manifestations of tolerance and love were conspicuous even during the period of the Crusades. This behavior continued unaltered even though Christendom had risen against the Islamic countries and had assaulted them with great fury. Ibn Jubayr says, "What is most curious about this period is the fact that Muslims and Christians were engaged in a deadly war, and on many occasions it has been witnessed that both armies were facing each other in perfect battle array. However, elsewhere the delegations of Muslims and Christians were moving from one place to another in perfect amity, and meeting with people, and nobody objected to this. The caravans were moving from Egypt to Damascus and from there to the European countries. Muslims were paying taxes to the Christians in their lands willingly, and the Christian traders were paying the custom duty for their merchandise in the Muslim countries, and full justice and equity was being observed in these dealings. While their armies are fighting with each other, the people were living in perfect amity and peace."

In short, the standard of religious tolerance in Islamic Civilization attained a height that has no parallel in history. Even the truth-loving historians of the West are in accord with this view and bear witness to it. The well known American writer, Draper, says, "During the period of the Caliphs, the learned men of the Christians and the Jews were not only held in great esteem but were appointed to posts of great responsibility and were promoted to the high ranking jobs in the government. Hārūn al-Rashīd appointed John, son of Masuyah as the Director of Public Instruction and all the schools and colleges were placed under his charge. Hārūn never took into account the country of origin or the faith that one belonged to. In fact, he did not take anything into consideration except one's excellence in the field of learning."

The well-known contemporary historian, Wells writes, "The Islamic teachings have left great traditions for equitable and gentle dealings and behavior and inspire people with nobility and tolerance. These are human teachings of the highest order and at the same time these teachings are practical. These teachings brought into existence a society in which hard-heartedness and collective oppression and injustice were at the lowest level when compared with all other societies preceding it." He continues, "Islam is replete with gentleness, tolerance and fraternity."

Sir Mark Syce, writing on the qualities of Muslim rule during the period of Hārūn al-Rashīd says, "The Christians, the polytheists, the Jews and Muslims were working equally in the Islamic State." Tirnun says, "Islam did not interfere in the affairs of the poets and the musicians."

Liefy Brutistal writes in his book, *Muslim Spain of the Tenth Century*: "So often the scribe writing out the terms of a treaty was a Jew or a Christian, just as many Jews and Christians were occupying important posts of the State. They were vested with authority in the administrative departments, even in matters of war and peace. Furthermore, there were several Jews who acted as the ambassadors of the Caliph in the European countries."

Reno writes in his book, *The History of Saracen Wars in France, Switzerland, Italy and Mediterranean Island*: "In Andalusian cities the Muslim meted out the best treatment to the Christians. Likewise, the Jews and the Christians had full regard for the feelings of Muslims. For example, they circumcized their offspring and abstained from eating pork."

Arnold, discussing the religious thought of the Christian religious sects writes, "The principles of Islamic religious tolerance do not allow such things which culminate in oppression and tyranny. Therefore, the behavior of Muslims remains quite different from that of the followers of other religions. Rather, Muslims did not approve of the injustices of the various sects of other religions which they had meted out to one another due to religious prejudices. This we can vouch for since we have before us the evidence of history which shows that where the various Christian sects living as subjects of the Islamic State were concerned, Muslims never faltered in the maintenance of the balance of justice between them. A manifest example of it is that after the conquest of Egypt, the Jacobite sect of the Christians took possession of their properties and churches by force to avenge themselves of the tyranny of the Byzantine Christians of the past. However, the Islamic State meted out full justice to them, and all the properties and churches of the conservative Christians to which they could prove their just claims were duly restored to them."

When one looks at the justice, equity and religious tolerance of Muslims to their Christian subjects in the early days of the Islamic State, it becomes very evident that the propaganda of the West regarding spread of Islam by the sword is not credible nor worthy of attention. In the present discourse on the theme of religious tolerance and freedom of religious thought in Islamic Civilization, detailed arguments and proofs have been cited so that the prejudiced historians may be fully exposed in their nonsensical accusation that Islam has been propagated and spread by the sword. It also shows that Muslims have not forced people to enter the fold of their faith and have not discriminated against non-Muslims.

It would have been better for these prejudiced historians not to have opened this door. Their dark history of fanaticism against Muslims in the Crusades and in Spain puts them to shame. No student of history dare deny their oppressive crimes even against one another. The Protestants killed and plundered the Catholics, and the bloodshed of St. Bartholomew is horrifying in its nature and magnitude. The wars that were waged between the supporters of the Papal Order and their adversaries, the European nations, are shameful. Likewise, during the Middle Ages, the barbarity of the officers of the Inquisition, who perpetrated oppression against the people, are in themselves extremely disgraceful. All these events are proof of the fact that European nations have a history of prejudice and an inability to tolerate any opinion against their own. Any alien creed, even if the contenders were their own countrymen and belonging to the same lineage, was not tolerated. During their history, not a single example of religious tolerance is on record.

Finally, the evidence of a great learned man and a leader of Christianity is presented. This testimony is from none other than the patriarch of Antioch, Michael, of the latter half of the twentieth century. Prior to this period, the Eastern Churches had been under Islamic rule for about five hundred years. This patriarch wrote about the religious tolerance of the Muslims and the oppression and tyranny of the Roman Christians perpetrated against the Eastern Churches. He goes on to say, "When God Almighty, the owner of all Power and the One who confers the rule of the land on whomsoever He pleases saw that the mischievous Christians of Rome, ravaging our [those of the Christians of Antioch] churches and plundering our homes on a large scale, He disgraced them. Divesting themselves of humanity, they inflicted the most grievous injury and torment on us. This was the time when God sent Banū Ismāʿīl from Arabia to release us from the painful torment in which Rome had placed us. Correct, we suffered some losses also due to the domination and authority of Muslims, such as the slipping away of several

Catholic Churches from our hands and going to the people of Khalqiduniah, but they had been in their possession for a long time. When the Muslim rule was established, whoever held a church was allowed to keep it. At that time we lost the Great Cathedral and the Church of Huran. However, compared with this petty loss it was a great advantage to be freed from the revenge of the Romans, their prejudice, their torments, their oppression and tyranny and live in the peace of Islam."

Gustav Le Bon writes, "History is not acquainted with any nation of conquerors, more kind-hearted and tolerant than the Arabs. Nor can history present any faith, so clear, simple, and harmless as that of the Arabs." This statement has done full justice to the truth.

CHAPTER SIX

MORALITY IN WAR

UNDER PEACEFUL AND secure conditions every nation can show courtesy, gentleness and kindness to the weak and the infirm, and adopt a tolerant attitude towards its neighbors. However, under conditions of war, to be just to people, to be gentle to the enemy, to have mercy on children, women and the old and to have compassion for the defeated nations is not something that every nation can do and few military leaders possess these traits. The sight of blood makes man's blood boil, and the inimical attitude of a nation creates malice and rouses rage in him. The intoxicating effect of conquest goes to the conqueror's head, and under these conditions he is at times guilty of the manifestation of the worst hard-heartedness and revenge. This is the history of nations, be they ancient or modern; in fact, it is the history of the whole world since Cain shed the blood of his brother Abel. The Quran says that they each offered a sacrifice, and it was accepted from the one of them and not accepted from the other. *[The other] said, "I will surely kill you." [The one] answered, "Allah accepts only from those who Fear Him"* (Quran, 5:27).

On this occasion of power, glory and war, history has placed the crown of eternal life on the heads of the leaders of civilization, whether they are soldiers, citizens, conquerors or rulers. Out of all civilizations, Islamic Civilization is the only one whose great men, even under the most difficult times, manifested the highest form of humanity based on justice and affection, particularly in situations where the circumstances roused men to bloodshed, oppression and revenge. If these Islamic morals of war had not been proved as undeniable historical events, it would have been regarded as a tale of something non-existent on this planet.

When Islam came to the world in its most perfect form, the world was functioning like a jungle. The mighty and remorseless murdered the weak and the armed man unhesitatingly robbed the unarmed of his belongings. Fighting was something usual in the lives of all faiths. And the religious laws, of nations and tribes, were not limited by any conditions nor confined to any limits. No distinction existed between the permissible and unlawful oppressive war. Whichever nation found itself powerful enough to snatch another nation's land, enslave its men and women, and compel it to abandon its creed and thought, did so without hesitation or guilt.

However, Islamic Civilization could not tolerate the idea that this tyrannical practice should continue in the world. Rather, it proclaimed to the world that in the matter of mutual relations between nations the real issue was recognition and co-operation. The Quran says, *O mankind! We created you from a single [pair] of a male and a female, and made you into nations and tribes so that you may know each other. Verily the most honored of you in the sight of Allah is [one who is] the most God-fearing of you* (Quran, 49:13).

The nation that does not want to live in peace and cannot rest without war with another nation forces the other nation to prepare itself to face the aggressive nation. The Quran says, *Against them make ready your strength to the utmost of your power, including steeds of war, to strike terror into the hearts of the enemies of Allah and your enemies* (Quran, 8:60).

If the aggressive nation desists from its aggressive stance, then the other nation must also extend its hand of friendship. It should show its desire for peace by every gesture. *But if the enemy incline towards peace, then incline towards peace, and put your trust in Allah* (Quran, 8:61).

But if the aggressive nation continues its aggression, then force needs to be met with force. The Quran says, *Fight in the cause of Allah those who fight you* (Quran, 2:190). These are the principles of Islamic Civilization which prohibits initiation of wars for the sake of booty, pillage and debasement of nations. The war, which is permitted, is only waged for any of the following objectives: 1) The protection of the morals and ideology of the people; and 2) the defence of the liberty, stability and security of a nation.

Allah says, *And fight them on until there is no more tumult or oppression, and religion is for Allah alone* (Quran, 2:193). For the nation declaring war in this situation, it is not enough that it safeguards its own freedom of belief; rather that it also safeguards the liberty of all other creeds and protects the places of worship of all religions. The Quran says, *Had it not been for Allah's checking some men by means of others, monasteries, churches, synagogues, and mosques, wherein the name of Allah is often mentioned, would have been destroyed* (Quran, 22:40).

Another brilliant aspect of Islamic Civilization in this regard, is that it protects the weak and oppressed groups of other nations in the same way that it protects the freedom and dignity of Muslims. The Quran says, *And why should you not fight in the cause of Allah while those oppressed among the men, women and children say, "Our Lord! Rescue us from this town whose people are oppressors! And give us from Your presence a protecting friend and give us from Your presence a defender!"* (Quran, 4:75).

Thus the war which is waged in defence of creed, freedom and peace is a legitimate war by which one can get closer to Allah and the martyrs are rewarded with Paradise. This is the war that Islamic Civilization has described as the "war for the sake of Allah," and is not a war based on tyranny and oppression. The difference between the legitimate war of Islamic Civilization and the wars known to other nations of the world has been beautifully brought out by the following verse of the Quran, *Those who believe fight in the cause of Allah, and those who reject faith fight in the cause of evil. So fight against the friends of Satan. Feeble indeed is the planning of Satan* (Quran, 4:76).

Islamic Civilization declares war to exalt the word of Allah and to establish the way of life suggested by the Quran. The system of Allah is good, the truth and honorable. As for the people, they only wage war for tyranny and Satan, and Satan is evil and sows mischief and corruption on earth. So when this is the reason behind the wars of Islamic Civilization—a war waged in the cause of truth and for the sake of good—it can never become the means of propagation of falsehood and evil. Thus one of the principles of Islam is that Muslims can and shall fight only against those who fight against them and oppress them. The Quran has laid down the following principle in this regard, *If anyone attacks you, attack him with the like of that with which he attacked you* (Quran, 2:194).

Therefore, if Muslims transgress these limits set by Allah and fight those who are not fighting and cause pain to those who inflict no pain, then they would become the transgressors deviating from the humane war and ideals. The Quran says, *Fight in the cause of Allah those who fight you, but do not transgress the limits; for Allah does not love transgressors* (Quran, 2:190).

In another place the Quran says, *But indeed if any do help and defend themselves after a wrong (done) to them, against such there is no cause of blame. The blame is only against those who oppress men with wrongdoing and insolently transgress beyond bounds through the land, defying right and justice, for such there will be a grievous penalty* (Quran, 42:41-42).

Once a war takes place against Muslims, it is their duty to abide by the principles of Islam, otherwise they will become corrupt, oppressive and destructive. It should never be allowed under any circumstances whatsoever. Since the war of humanity is in the way of Allah alone, even from the aspect of the means at the disposal of Muslims, it should remain restricted to limits of humanity, however fierce and violent that war may be.

That is why the instructions given by Islam in connection

with war are not to be found in the history of any other civilization. Abū Bakr the first Caliph of the Prophet issued the following instructions to the army led by Usāma: "Do not mutilate and disfigure your enemies after you have killed them. Do not kill children, old people or women. Do not destroy the palm tress or burn them. Do not cut down a tree bearing fruits. Slaughter only as many animals as you actually need for your food. You will come upon people who have devoted themselves to churches and monasteries. Leave them alone and let them pursue the mission for which they have renounced the world."

Such are the features of a humane war that it is waged for the cause of Allah and not for evil and enmity. Such a war is restricted by these principles of mercy, until either of two things take place: peace or victory. In case of a treaty, its terms are strictly adhered to and are binding. As Allah says, *Fulfil the covenant of Allah when you have entered into it, and break not your oaths after you have confirmed them, indeed you have made Allah your surety* (Quran, 16:91).

As for victory, it is the victory of a party that has strived for the Truth and its individuals became martyrs in the way of Allah. Such a party takes only those steps after victory which make the roots of the order of Truth firmer in the land and puts an end to corruption and oppression among the people. The Quran says, *They are those who, if we establish them in the land, establish regular Prayer and give regular Zakāt, enjoin the right and forbid the wrong. With Allah rests the end [and decision] of [all] affairs* (Quran, 22:41).

These are the limits prescribed by Islamic Civilization for the activities of its conqueror—spiritualism, social justice, cooperation in deeds of righteousness, general welfare and ceaseless struggle against evil and mischief. These are the principles and elements of war of Islamic Civilization—justice, mercy and fulfilment of covenants.

What has been said so far, is not sufficient as evidence of the morality in war found in Islamic Civilization since the mere presentation of principles and their general proclamation are not enough proof of the eminence and the philanthropy of a nation. The world has witnessed many nations that come forward before the world with very lofty and sublime objectives, but their behavior towards other nations is disgraceful, cruel and far from the humane principles of mercy and justice. The game played by the colonial powers in the Muslim countries is no secret, nor is the history of their shameful and cruel deeds hidden. Therefore, it becomes important to look closely at the practical implementation of these principles during the peak of Islamic Civilization. This is the point where disgrace is the portion of some nations and others are honored. It is here that Islamic Civilization becomes distinguished from all other civilizations and none can match the philanthropy of Islamic Civilization in times of war.

One should begin with examples from the life of the Messenger of Allah since he is the founder of Islamic Civilization and it is he who laid down its principles and regulations. It is he who is competent to interpret the aims, means and features of Islamic Civilization correctly. The history of the Prophets and the reformers makes it evident that no other Prophet had to face such torment and hardship in the way of his call to the truth in quantity or quality as was confronted patiently by the Messenger of Allah. His Makkan life, spread over thirteen long years of suffering, is known to all. During this whole period, both he and his party of believers had to face the malice, enmity, torments, reproach and revilement of the opponents, so much so that attempts were made on his own life and those of his Companions. After that, even a cursory glance at his ten years of life in Madinah reveals that this entire period was occupied by struggle and constant *Jihād*. He could not completely discard his armour until a short while before his passing away, when the entire Arabian Peninsula had become dominated by him. It has been generally observed that those who have constantly been a prey to enmities, oppression, tyranny and conspiracies become avengeful; and, when they enter the battlefield and they lift the sword and come to grips with the enemy, their nature becomes ferocious and cruel. Note the moral behavior demonstrated by the Prophet in all those wars actually forced upon him, and note how he practically demonstrated the principles of war of Islamic Civilization as proclaimed by him.

During the Battle of Uḥud, due to the violation of the instructions of the Prophet, the believers were confronted with a setback and the enemies surrounded him, and in order to put an end to his life they fell upon him from all sides. He was wounded, one of his teeth was broken, his face was injured and one of the rings of his helmet was embedded in his cheek. His Companions put their own lives at risk to defend him against the enemies and rescued him from their attack. At this juncture some of his Companions requested him to curse the enemies.

He said in reply, "Allah did not send me to reproach [and curse] people but as a mercy to them and as one calling them to the truth....O Allah! Guide my nation for they do not know." This is the logic of truth that forces one to war, and this is the logic of the Prophet ﷺ who does not fight to shed blood but to guide the misguided.

It was also in the battle of Uḥud that the lion of Allah—Ḥamza—was killed. Ḥamza was the Prophet's uncle and one of the most outstanding heroes of Arabia. He was killed by someone named Waḥshī at the instigation of Hind, the wife of Abū Sufyān. When Ḥamza became a martyr in the battlefield, Hind searched for his dead body and upon finding it she took out the heart and liver and started to eat them. Later, both Hind and Waḥshī embraced Islam. How then did the Messenger of Allah treat them? He forgave Hind and accepted Waḥshī into the fold of Islam saying, "If you can live far away from us then do so." This is how the Messenger of Allah dealt with his uncle's killer and mutilator.

In one of the battles, the Prophet ﷺ found a woman who had been killed. He was very angry and said, "Did I not prohibit the killing of women in battle? She was not fighting against you." This is the Messenger of Allah who is giving a lesson in humanity even in the battlefield, thus giving a practical demonstration of his instructions relating to war.

When the Messenger of Allah conquered Makkah and entered it, at the head of ten thousand soldiers, the Quraysh surrendered. They all waited at the doors of the Kaʿbah waiting for the judgment of the Messenger of Allah whom they had fought for twenty-one years. The Messenger of Allah asked them, "O people of Quraysh! What do you think I am going to do with you?" They said in reply, "We expect extremely benevolent treatment from you. You are a noble brother and the son of a noble brother." To this he replied, "I will say the same to you that Yūsuf had said to his brothers, *This day let no reproach be (cast) on you. Allah will forgive you, and he is the Most Merciful of those who show mercy.* Go, you are all free!" This is Muḥammad the Messenger of Allah, teacher of all goodness to mankind, a leader who was not bloodthirsty in waging wars, and was not intoxicated with military successes.

After the period of the Messenger of Allah, his Companions and Caliphs displayed the same degree of morality in wars and conquests, and implemented the principles of Islamic Civilization. Under the most difficult conditions and at the most critical stages, they kept themselves under control and even after the greatest victories they did not forget their principles.

Some inhabitants of Lebanon rose in revolt against the governor ʿAlī ibn ʿAbdullāh ibn ʿAbbās. He fought against them and defeated them. He deemed it fit not to allow the rebels another chance to join forces and rise against him and decided to disperse and deport some of them. However Imām al-Awzāʿī, the great scholar wrote to him saying that his action would go against Islamic law. He mentioned that to punish others along with those who took part in the rebellion and deporting them could not be permitted. Only the guilty could be punished. He wrote, "It has come to my knowledge that you have executed some people of *dhimmah* [non-Muslims who live under Islamic rule paying a tax in return for their security and freedom] of the Lebanese mountains and others you have deported. Some of the exiled are those who did not co-operate with the rebels. Let me know under which principle you are punishing the people in general for the sins of a particular person or a group. You are turning them out of their homes and sending them away from their properties, whereas Allah has ordained that no bearer of burdens can bear the burden of another. This is the best stand and worth pursuing. Also the following injunction of the Prophet ﷺ must always be kept in view, 'Whoever oppresses a person living under guarantee of protection by the Islamic State or burdenes him with a burden beyond his capacity, I shall uphold his case on the Day of Reckoning.'" (Abū Dāwūd) The governor had no option but to repatriate the deported people to their homes and villages with dignity and honor.

It would be apt at this juncture to remind people of the behavior of the French towards Muslims during their struggle for freedom, when they were occupying the Muslim lands of North Africa. They killed tens of thousands, razed so many cities and towns to the ground, and they present an appearance of wilderness where it seems nobody ever lived. One also needs to remind people of the barbaric treatment of the Arabs at the hands of the British during their struggle for the freedom of Palestine.

When ʿUmar ibn ʿAbd al-ʿAzīz assumed the office of Caliphate, a delegation from Samarqand came and complained to him about the General of the Islamic army, Quṭaybah, who had unjustifiably entered their city and stationed his soldiers in the town. ʿUmar ibn ʿAbd al-ʿAzīz wrote to the governor of

Samarqand and advised him to appoint a tribunal to judge and settle the dispute between Quṭaybah and the people of Samarqand. If the judgment of the tribunal goes against the general and his men are asked to vacate, they must do so at once. The governor appointed Jāmiᶜ ibn Hadhir al-Bājī as judge. After the enquiry, he passed judgment that the Muslim army must vacate the town. He also remarked that the commander of the Muslim forces ought to have served an ultimatum of war to the city, and according to Islamic Law relating to war, he ought to have cancelled all the treaties with them so that the people of Samarqand could have had time to prepare for the war. Sudden attack on them without warning was unlawful.

When the people of Samarqand witnessed this state of affairs, they were convinced that this was an unparallel case in the history of mankind where justice was being implemented by the State on its arm and its leaders. Consequently they decided that fighting against such a people would be futile. Rather, they came to regard it as mercy and a blessing from Allah. Therefore, they agreed to live with the Muslim army in Samarqand.

Imagine this! An army conquers a city and enters it. The inhabitants of that city complain to the victorious government, and the judges of that government decide the case against the victorious army and order its extradition saying that they could not live there without the consent of the people of that city. Can either the ancient or modern history of mankind point out any war in which the fighting men kept themselves so strictly bound by a moral code and followed such lofty principles of truth and justice as demonstrated by the army of Islamic Civilization? In so far as the author's knowledge is concerned, not one nation of the world can be pointed out which demonstrated such lofty morals.

The armies of Islamic Civilization conquered Damascus, Ḥums and the remaining towns of Syria, and according to the terms of the treaty they collected an amount of tax for the protection of the life and property of the citizens and the defence of the country. Later the Muslim leaders received news that Heraclius had brought a big army and was anxious to fight the Muslims. The Muslim army decided to bring together their own scattered armies in various conquered towns to collectively face the enemy. So in keeping with this decision, the Muslim armies started leaving Ḥums, Damascus and other towns. Khālid in Ḥums, Abū ʿUbayda in Damascus and other generals in other towns addressed the citizens thus, "We have taken your money so that we may protect your lives and properties and to defend your lands from outside aggression. But now we are leaving you and thus will not be able to protect you. Here are the taxes you have paid, we are returning them to you!" To this the citizens said in reply, "May Allah be with you and bring you back victorious. By Allah, your governance and your justice is dearer to us than the injustice and oppression of the Romans. By Allah, if they were in your place, they would not have returned anything that they would have taken from us. Rather, they would have taken everything they could possibly carry!"

Even in the so-called civilized period of today, if the armies have to vacate a station, they do not leave there anything that the enemy could utilize to their advantage. Is there a single example of the practice of the victorious armies of Islamic Civilization in the entire history of mankind? By Allah! If one had no faith in lofty values, and did not believe in their success, or, like the politicians of the modern age, considered it necessary to keep morals and principles dominated by political interests, one would have said that the leaders of the Muslims armies stuck to lofty values and abided by moral principles due to their unawareness and simplicity. Yet it is a fact that they were really true believers and did not like to say things they could not put into practice.

When the Tartars made a sudden assault on Syria and took countless Muslims, Jews and Christians as prisoners, Shaykh al-Islām ibn Taymiyyah intervened and talked with the leader of the Tartars about the release of the prisoners. The Tartar leader gave his assent for the release of the Muslim prisoners but refused to do so in the case of the Jews and the Christians. But Shaykh al-Islām did not agree and said to him, "You have to release the Jews and the Christians who are the *Dhimmīs* of the Islamic State. We cannot let even one individual remain in captivity whether they are from our community or from among those who live with us under a covenant."

Contrary to this, one has only to look at what the Crusaders did during the Crusades. During the Middle Ages when these wars were thrust on Muslims, Muslims fulfilled the covenants, while the Christian Crusaders never let a chance of treachery slip by. Muslims habitually overlooked their mischief but the Crusaders always took revenge. Muslims were careful to save human life as much as possible but the Crusaders shed so much blood that it ran into knee-deep pools. Yet these merciless brutes prided in their shameful deeds, rejoiced and gloated over them.

When the Crusaders reached Ma'rah al-Nuʿmān in their second onslaught, the inmates were compelled to lay down their arms. However, before surrendering the town to the enemy they made the responsible leaders of the invaders guarantee the safety of their lives and property. What actually happened? Upon entering the city they perpetrated such crimes of cruelty, oppression and tyranny whose dreadfulness would make the children old. Some English historians who participated in this war have stated that the number of those slain was a hundred thousand souls, young and old, men and women.

After this the enemy advanced towards Bayt al-Maqdis and besieged the civilian population. Fully convinced that they would be vanquished, they took a pledge from the supreme commander of the invading armies, Tankard, for the protection of their lives and properties. He gave the citizens a white banner to be hoisted over the Aqṣā Mosque and advised them to enter that haven for their safety. They were assured of the safety of everything. The invaders entered the town. What horror this sacred city was faced with; what horrid crimes were perpetrated!

The citizens of Bayt al-Maqdis took refuge in the Aqṣā Mosque, on which the banner given to them by Tankard was hoisted according to his instructions. This sacred Mosque was packed to capacity with old men, women and children. Those who had plighted their word to protect their lives and properties and given them the banner of peace entered the holy mosque and slaughtered all those frail and defenceless old men, children and women like goats and sheep. The place of worship was filled with human blood which reached the knees of the horsemen.

Thus in slaughtering the citizens, they sanctified the city, according to their own mode of thinking, and washed it with blood. The public highways and streets were littered with human skulls. Everywhere amputated limbs, severed organs and deformed bodies were lying with no one to mourn or bury them. Men of the Muslim armies have stated that in the Aqṣā mosque alone, seventy thousand people were slaughtered, among whom, apart from women and children, there was a large number of learned men and devout persons. The English historians too have not denied these shameful deeds of their co-religionists. Instead, they stated these feats with great pride.

Ninety years after this dreadful slaughter and bloodshed, Ṣalāḥuddīn al-Ayyūbī conquered Bayt al-Maqdis. And what did he do with the inhabitants of this sanctum? More than a hundred thousand Christians lived there and the conqueror guaranteed security of life and property to them and took a small amount, not from every one, but only from those who could easily pay it and allowed them to leave the town. They were also given respite for forty days for preparation before departure. In this way, eighty-four thousand people left the town in perfect safety. Many went to ʿAkka and other towns to their friends, relatives and co-religionists. A large number of them were exempted from payment of the *jizyah* [protection money payable to the Islamic State by non-Muslim citizens] and Ṣalāḥuddīn's brother Mālik ʿĀdil paid the *jizyah* for two thousand people from his own pocket. The treatment meted out to the women was far from what would be expected of a conqueror today. When the Christian patriarch wanted to leave the place, Ṣalāḥuddīn permitted him to do so. The Christian patriarch had much wealth amassed through churches, synagogues, the Ṣakhra and Aqṣā mosques, and ceremonies, and some counsellors advised Ṣalāḥuddīn to confiscate his wealth, but Ṣalāḥuddīn told them that he could not go back upon his word. He took from him the same amount of *jizyah* as he had taken from the ordinary people. However, what increased his honor and glory on the occasion of the conquest of Bayt al-Maqdis was his mode of action in the process of evacuation of the Christians of the sanctum. He provided guards for the safe transit of the evacuees and the escorts had instructions to take them to the Christian habitations of Saur and Saida to their co-religionists in perfect safety. All this whilst the Christian world was still at war with Muslims. It seems unimaginable.

Furthermore, there were several women who had paid the *jizyah* and who came to Ṣalāḥuddīn stating that their husbands, fathers and sons had either been killed in the battle or were in captivity. They had no one to look after them, nor was there any place where they could seek shelter. They were weeping and wailing. Seeing them tearful, the tender-hearted Ṣalāḥuddīn burst into tears himself. He ordered, after an enquiry to discover the whereabouts of the husbands, sons and fathers of the women, that the captives should be released and those whose guardians had been killed be given generous compensation. These women, wherever they went, praised Ṣalāḥuddīn loudly and when, after scrutiny, the prisoners were released, they were also permitted to go to Saur, ʿAkka and other places to their co-religionists.

As for the Christian evacuees from Bayt al-Maqdis, they went to their brethren in nearby towns. Some of them went to Antioch, but the Christian leader of that city refused entry to them. They went about wandering in search of shelter and support, and finally it was Muslims who offered them refuge. One contingent went to Tripoli, which was governed by Latin rulers, but even they did not allow them entry and drove them away from their premises after robbing them of all their worldly goods they had been allowed to take with them by the Muslims.

Ṣalāḥuddīn's benevolent treatment of the Christians during the Crusades *prima facie* seems to be a tale. If the Western writers had not been amazed at the noble nature and lofty morals of this great hero of Islam, the world would have certainly found room to accuse Muslims historians of exaggeration. The Western historians themselves mention the event when Ṣalāḥuddīn learnt of the illness of Richard, the greatest and the most valiant general of the Crusaders—he sent his personal physician for his treatment and also sent him such fruits that were not easily available at that time of the year. This happened while hostilities were on in full fury, and the armies of both parties were engaged in a life and death struggle. The Western historians also mention that a woman approached the camp of Ṣalāḥuddīn, and wailing and weeping she complained to him that her child had been snatched away from her by two Abyssinian soldiers. Ṣalāḥuddīn himself was moved to tears by the pitiable condition of the woman, and there and then, appointed a military officer to make enquires. The child was found and returned to its mother. She was then escorted to her camp at his bidding. Dare any one say in face of all this evidence that the morality of Islamic Civilization, relating to fighting forces and in times wars, is not humane!

When Sultan Muḥammad II conquered Constantinople he entered the cathedral of St. Sophia where all the priests had gathered to seek refuge. He met them very courteously and assured them that he would support every reasonable request from them, and they had no reason to be frightened. Those who had sought shelter there out of fear, should rest assured and return to their homes with an easy conscience. Later Muḥammad II attended to the various problems of the Christians and solved them. He gave them assurance that they could follow their personal laws, religious obligations, and the customs of their particular churches. In addition, he authorized the priests to freely elect their bishop. They elected Jenadeus. On this occasion, the Sultan also ordered celebrations with great pomp and show, which were usually made during the Byzantine rule. He said to the bishop that in his capacity as a bishop, he was his friend at all times and at all places, and he should derive full benefit of all those rights and privileges his predecessors had enjoyed. After that, the Sultan offered him a beautiful steed as a gift and gave him one of his bodyguards for his protection, and high-ranking government officials escorted him to the palace which the Sultan had built for him. The Sultan then proclaimed that he had sanctioned the laws of the Orthodox Church and the patriarch should protect them. He purchased all the goods of archaeological interest and abandoned articles picked up by the people on the occasion of the conquest and restored them to the churches and to other institutions.

Sultan Muḥammad meted out this treatment to the Christians even though there was no treaty between him and the Christians at the time of the conquest of Constantinople that he might have been obliged to fulfil. He kindly offered this privilege and support purely on grounds of his generosity and benevolent nature. It was due to this kind treatment of his that the people of Constantinople felt that under the new Islamic regime, they were living in greater peace and religious freedom than under their former Byzantine rulers.

Similarly, the Ottoman rulers continued with kind treatment of their Christian subjects in the conquered neighboring lands. In the Bulgarian and the Greek states, such treatment was not meted out to them anywhere in Europe itself. It was so benevolent that in Hungary and Transylvania, the followers of Cliffon and the Unitarian Christians of Transylvania chose to live under the Turkish authority instead of submitting themselves to the tyrannical rule of the extremely bigoted sect of Christians of the house of Habsburg. The Protestant sects of Silesia longed to attain religious freedom under the Muslim rule.

At the time when this kind and noble treatment was meted out to the Christians under the Turkish rule, religious prejudices were at their height. The prejudiced rulers were oppressing sects other than their own. Other religious sects too were at war with one another, blood was being freely shed and there was no security of life. During the seventh century, the patriarch of Antioch, Maccarios, writing about the tyrannies of the Roman Catholic sects of Poland perpetrated against the orthodox sects, said, "We bitterly mourn the loss of those thousands of martyrs who have been murdered by the cruel Roman Catholic infidels and enemies of the faith during the last forty or fifty years and whose number approaches seventy thousand. O you traitors! O you unholy sinners! O you hardhearted creatures! I ask you what was the fault of the nuns worshipping in the churches? Why did you put them to the sword? For what crime were the young women and small children killed? Why should I not call them the accursed and damned souls of Poland when they have proved themselves more debased and cruel than the mischief-making idolaters perpetrating cruelty on Christians. In oppressing the Christians they were laboring under the erroneous notion that they would be able to efface the orthodox church altogether. God in His infinite Mercy preserves the Turkish government for all time to come. They take the *jizyah* and have no ill will against other religions whether they are Christians, Nazarenes, Jews or Samaritans. But the damned Polish ones did not stop at taking taxes; and in spite of the fact that the Christians were willingly prepared to serve them, they handed over the Christians to the cruel Jews who are enemies of the Christians at heart. They did not permit the Christians to build even one church, nor left alive any priest among them who could teach them their faith."

The generous treatment meted out by Sultan Muḥammad to the Christians attached to the Cathedral of St. Sophia and the benevolence with which he granted rights to the Christians of Constantinople was so different. This came at a time when European Christians treated their own brethren, the Orthodox Christians, when they conquered Constantinople in 1204 AD, in a despicable manner. Pope Innocent III said, "The duty of the followers of Jesus and the supporters of his faith was to turn the edges of their swords towards the greatest enemy of Christianity [Islam]. But it is a pity Christians shed the blood of the Christians themselves, which was religiously forbidden to them. But they did not care at all for it, and shed much blood. They neither respected the faith, nor discriminated between the sexes nor had they any regard for age, or youth in this bloodshed. They committed fornication and adultery in broad daylight, and the nuns, mothers of children and virgins found themselves equally helpless before these lustful creatures; and the sensual beasts of this army devoured them. These robbers and plunderers did not stop at robbing the king and other aristocrats of their riches, but ravaged and plundered the lands and other properties of the churches. They desecrated the churches also, robbing them of the sacred portraits, crosses and holy relics."

The well-known historian Charles Dale writes, "This [Christian] army, intoxicated with power, entered the Cathedral of St. Sophia, destroyed the holy books and trampled portraits of the martyrs under foot. A corrupt woman was occupying the chair of the patriarch, and she started singing loudly. All traces of religious knowledge were effaced from the city, and the gold and silver statues were destroyed to provide material for their gold and silver coins." The monks who were eye-witnesses to these painful scenes acknowledged that "the followers of Muḥammad had never dealt with the inhabitant of this city as the soldiers of Christ had dealt with them."

Yes. Muslims certainly did not do any such things when they

conquered Constantinople, as witnessed by the behavior of Sultan Muḥammad. Muslims, so long as they were believers, could not manifest narrow-mindedness and even approach such shameful deeds of religious bigotry as perpetrated by the Roman Catholic followers of Christ against other Christians.

One need not take up in detail the story of the Muslim conquerors of Andalusia and their generous treatment of the minorities of that country. Neither need one take up in detail their affectionate behavior and extreme regard for their feelings and compare it with the treatment Muslims met at the hands of the Spaniards when they took over the last surviving Muslim state of Granada. They did all that despite the treaty with Muslims which comprised about sixty provisions, about the protection of their faith, their mosques, their honor, dignity and their properties and so many other things. However, they did not fulfil any of their pledges, nor met any responsibility in this behalf. Rather, they did not desist even from the murder of innocent people and took possession of their properties. Again, within thirty years of the fall of Granada, Europe declared in 1534 CE that all the mosques be converted into churches. So one finds that within four years of this declaration Muslims were totally wiped out in Spain. This is how the Christians fulfilled their side of the treaty and this is how Muslims fulfilled their side.

What amazes us is the fact that they behaved in this cruel manner and were guilty of the breach of contract with their own co-religionists. This oppression and cruelty was no less than that perpetrated against Muslims. Wherever they went as conquerors, they implemented the same hardheartedness, oppression and tyranny. Be it in the East or West, they always appeared in their true colors as cunning and cruel, no matter whether their prey was some weak Muslim or a Christian. Their writers themselves lament their national character. The Priest Ododvalley, a courtier of Louis Vil, in favor with him, and having participated in the Second Crusade with the king, wrote, "When the Christians were going to Bayt al-Maqdis through Asia Minor, they suffered a great defeat at the hands of the Turks in the mountainous region of Frigia. That was in 1148 CE. With great difficulty they got to a coastal town of Italy. Here, those who could meet the heavy demands of the Greeks [they took the armies across the sea] reached Antioch by the sea route. Yet they left behind their sick, wounded and ordinary people at the mercy of their perfidious Greek allies. Louis paid the Greeks five hundred marks for their protection and the treatment of the disabled and the sick, so that they might be able to join their companions. Hardly had the army left Italy when the Greeks informed the Turks of the presence of these unarmed Crusaders, and quietly waited to watch the fun of these wretched people facing starvation, disease and above all the spears of the enemy. This death and destruction came upon them when they were proceeding towards their cantonment. Four thousand individuals out of this unarmed and disabled multitude in desperation tried to escape this tragic end. The Turkish army that had returned to the cantonment turned round with the idea of taking their victory to a conclusive end and routed and ruined this army. Those who escaped this calamity were despairing of their lives. The Muslims were greatly moved by their pitiable plight, and instead of enmity their hearts were now filled with affection for them. They nursed the sick and helped the hungry and the destitute who were at the verge of death and destruction. The Muslims extended their generosity to the extent of purchasing the cash in French currency from the Greeks who had snatched it from them, and gave it to these wretched travellers. There was a world of difference between the cruel and beastly behavior of their own Greek Christian brethren with these travellers and the just and merciful treatment of the heathens [Muslims]. The Greeks played a dirty joke on them, beat them and whatever Louis had left for their maintenance, they robbed them of it all. This resulted in some of them entering the fold of the faith of their saviours willingly, as attested by one of our historians of the past, 'Their own cruel brothers oppressed them but the disbelievers [Muslims] offered them security and shelter and most benevolent treatment.' We learn that more than three thousand of those returning alive joined the Turks. Alas! This kindness and mercy was more disagreeable than treachery. They certainly gave them bread but snatched their faith and beliefs from them. Although it is true that they did not compel any one to abandon his faith, but confined their efforts to service and benevolence to them."

We need not look too far for evidence. The impressions and record of the cruelties of the Western nations in the two World Wars and their morals and deeds in the Islamic Middle East serve as clear evidence that in governance and in the battlefield their conduct has been extremely tyrannical and a model of barbarism. Their hypocritical policy is no longer a secret, though they continue to let loose their loud propaganda about their civilization, culture, philanthropy, love and affection. However, in their wars, in their dominions and colonies, they openly demonstrate their barbarism and bloodthirstiness. Some people offer the excuse for this mode of action from the Western nations that during the Middle Ages they were not so civilized and cultured; thus any other behavior could not be expected of them. A very pertinent question is that now that they are civilized and claim to benefit the whole world with sciences and arts and new inventions, are they any better? According to objective analysis, the problem really is, 'What is their true temperament which overwhelms every effort of theirs at affectation and hypocrisy?' The fact of the matter is that the Western nations still have those traits and habits of the days of their barbarity and idolatry in their entirety. During the Middle Ages these traits and habits took the shape of religious prejudice, so religion had to bear the brunt of their barbarity. Today the same cruel and barbaric habits are at work under the garb of civilization and peace; security and civilization have to bear the burden of their hard-heartedness and inhumanity. In fact in every period these nations have been mischief-makers, cruel, blood-thirsty, lovers of power and authority and bigoted and barbaric. How then dare they tell tales of the hard-heartedness under Islamic victories and present their despicable colonialism as a mercy and kindness? The situation is as the poet says:

When we were in power, forgiveness was our known habit.
But when you came to rule you shed rivers of (much) blood.
This difference between the two of us is not much.
Since whatever are the contents of a vessel, spill out of it.

CHAPTER SEVEN

COMPASSION AND KINDNESS TO ANIMALS

THIS IS REALLY a strange topic of discourse to be included within the topic of glory of Islamic Civilization, although in this day and age it may not be considered as a novelty. Until recently, humanity could not imagine that animals could also be deserving of mercy and justice. Even today nations kill animals as a recreational activity on occasions of sport, celebrations and festivals. However, in this field as well, Islamic Civilization presents itself as a messenger of human consciousness and is unlike any other past or present civilization when it comes to kind treatment and mercy to animals. This has been so well established that it cannot be overlooked, and it will amaze and fascinate everyone who was not aware of this particular aspect of the Islamic Civilisation.

Islam views the animal world as a world in its own right, just like that of the human world, with its own characteristics, temperaments and feelings. The Quran says, *There is not an animal [that lives] on earth, nor a being that flies on its wings, but [forms part] of communities like you* (Quran, 6:38).

Since they are a community like mankind, they too deserve mercy and affection. The Prophet ﷺ said, "The Merciful showers mercy on those who are themselves merciful" (Aḥmad). He also said, "One who has been endowed with a gentle nature has received a portion of the goodness of this world and the next" (Aḥmad).

Kindness to animals may at times become the reason for which one is rewarded with Paradise. The Prophet ﷺ is reported to have said, "A person was walking when he felt very thirsty. He came upon a well. He went down the well and quenched his thirst. On coming up he saw a dog panting and witnessed its extreme thirst as it licked the moist earth around the well. He thought to himself that the dog was also dying of thirst just as he had been. So he went down the well once again and filled one of his leather stockings with water and held it with his teeth. When he came up he offered that water to the dog. Allah looked with favor on this act of kindness and forgave him his sins." Someone from the audience asked him, "O Messenger of Allah! Will we be rewarded for kindness to animals also?" He replied, "You will be rewarded for kind treatment of all those having a liver [living] and subsisting on fodder [feed of some sort]" (Bukhārī and Muslim).

In fact, cruelty to animals can place a person in Hell. "A certain woman entered Hell due to a cat that she kept tied in her house, neither feeding it nor freeing it to seek its food among the vermin of the earth" (Bukhārī).

The *Sharīʿah* has also prescribed legislation regarding compassion to animals. It is prohibited to mount an animal for a long period of time whilst it is standing still. The Messenger of Allah ﷺ said, "Do not take the backs of your animals as chairs" (Aḥmad).

Similarly, it has been prohibited to starve animals, expose them to weakness and keep them in a poor condition. Once the Messenger of Allah ﷺ happened to pass by a camel whose empty stomach was touching its back. At this he said, "Do fear Allah in the matter of these dumb creatures. Use them for riding only when they are in a fit condition and leave them [to rest] from work while they yet have some energy left in them."

It is also not permitted to make animals work beyond their capacity. The Messenger of Allah once entered the garden of one of the Anṣār. There he saw a camel. On looking at the Prophet ﷺ, the camel began to moan piteously and tears welled up in its eyes. The Prophet ﷺ approached the camel, wiped its tears and then asked, "Who is the owner of this camel?" The owner said, "It is I, O Messenger of Allah!" The Prophet said to him, "Do you have any fear of Allah in relation to this animal which Allah has given you? It complained to me that you keep it hungry yet overwork it" (Aḥmad).

Wanton killing of animals for fun and sport has been strictly prohibited. The Prophet ﷺ has said, "Whoever kills even one bird wantonly, it will complain to Allah on the Day of Judgment, 'O my Lord and Cherisher! This person had killed me in vain and not for any benefit'" (Nasā'ī).

Likewise, using animals as targets for practice is also prohibited. The Prophet ﷺ has cursed the person who uses a living object as a target [for practice] (Bukhārī and Muslim).

The *Sharīʿah* has prohibited making animals fight and has also prohibited branding [with hot irons for the sake of distinction]. The Prophet ﷺ passed by a donkey that had been branded on the face, and said, "May Allah curse the person who did it." If the animal is to be slaughtered for food, kindness demands that a very sharp knife be used for its slaughtering. The animal should be offered water to drink, and after the slaughtering, the carcass should be allowed to cool down before skinning. The Prophet ﷺ is reported to have said, "Allah has proscribed perfection in everything, thus if you kill, then make perfect the killing and if you slaughter, then make perfect the slaughtering. Let each one of you sharpen his blade and put the slaughtered animal at rest" (Muslim).

So much care has been exercised in this matter, such that sharpening the knife in front of the animal that is about to be slaughtered has been considered as a form of cruelty and hard-heartedness. The Prophet ﷺ saw somebody sharpening his knife in front of the goat he was going to slaughter, and said to him, "Do you want to slaughter it many times?" And then added, "Why did you not sharpen your knife beforehand?"

The following incident is very touching when it comes to kindness to animals and shows the spirit of the Islamic Civilization. ʿAbdullāh ibn Masʿūd said, "We were on a journey with the Messenger of Allah, when we saw a sparrow that had two fledglings with it. We caught both of them. The mother was hovering over our heads. When the Prophet ﷺ came, he asked, 'Who has troubled this bird by snatching from it its young ones? Return her fledglings to her.' On the same journey the Prophet

ﷺ observed that setting fire to an anthill had destroyed it, and said, 'Who burnt it?' We said, 'We did.' He said, 'No one has the right to punish by fire except the Lord of fire'" (Abū Dāwūd).

In the light of these teachings, Muslim jurists have made laws relating to the kind treatment of animals. The jurists say that it is imperative for the owner of animals to provide for all their needs. If he does not do so, he will be forced to sell them, spend money on them, let them loose in the wilderness where they can find food and shelter, or slaughter them if their meat is permitted as food. Some jurists have gone further and said, "If a blind cat enters somebody's house and is unable to move about to seek its food, it becomes incumbent on the householders to feed it." The jurists have also prohibited people from putting greater burden on animals than they can easily bear. Following on from this principle, they have deduced several legal rights. Thus if someone hires an animal and loads it with a burden heavier than its capacity and thus causes its death, he becomes liable to pay damages for it.

Similarly the jurists have also determined the amount of weight which can be loaded on the mule and the donkey. It is interesting to note that once a certain jurist determined the quantity that can be loaded on the donkey and the mule, but another jurist did not agree with him and said, "In prescribing this amount, justice has been done to the mule but great injustice has been done to the donkey." However, if an animal harms another, it will not be punished for its act. Rather, the owner would be liable if it can be proved that he had been careless in looking after the animal and restraining it from causing harm.

These are the principles of kindness and mercy shown towards animals of the Islamic Civilization and the *Sharīʿah*. How then were these principles applied and transformed into practice?

While the Messenger of Allah was on a journey, he heard an Anṣārī woman cursing the camel that she was riding. The Messenger of Allah rejected such an attitude and said, "Remove whatever is on the camel's back and release it as it has been cursed [i.e. humiliated by its owner]." The camel was thus left to roam about freely without anyone troubling it (Muslim).

ʿUmar ibn al-Khaṭṭāb saw a person dragging a goat by its leg to slaughter it. He said to him, "Woe unto you. If you take the animal to its death, do so in a beautiful manner."

This was the kind treatment and tender-heartedness which was meted out to animals by the Islamic State and other welfare institutions of Islamic Civilization. Proof of the importance that the Islamic State attached to the kind treatment of animals can be reinforced by the fact that the Caliph issued instructions to the common people not to cause animals hardship nor trouble them, but to treat them kindly. In a letter, ʿUmar ibn ʿAbd al-ʿAzīz instructed the governors to prevent people from racing horses without any right. He wrote to the officer in charge of the traffic police and patrolling body that he should not allow anybody to put a heavy bridle on the animal nor use whips with an iron piece at their end. The duties of the patrol officers included prohibiting people from putting very heavy loads on the animals or inflicting injuries and torturing animals unnecessarily during a journey. The law in this regard is as follows: "The patrol officer has the right to use his authority to compel people to comply with the rules and regulation in this behalf, since they imply general expediency. People should not be allowed to load their animals with loads heavier than their capacity, nor can they be permitted to goad them to great speed when they are carrying heavy loads. They should be made to desist from beating them. They should not tie their animals in public parks either. All these practices are against the Islamic *Sharīʿah*. It is the duty of the owners of the animals to be God-fearing in the matter of their feed. The fodder should be enough to fully satisfy the animals' hunger. It should be neither of a poor quality nor meagre in quantity."

The welfare institutions of the Islamic State also catered for animals. The best proof of this is furnished by those documents of the trusts of the past, which were concerned only with the treatment of sick animals. There were also land trusts that were meant solely for the arrangement of the grazing of old disabled animals. One of these is the *al-Marj al-Akhḍar* of Damascus which was converted into a playground by the Municipal Corporation. This pasture was a trust for the horses abandoned as useless by their owners. They would graze in it until they died. One of the trusts of Damascus was meant exclusively for cats. These cats were provided with food and shelter and in this way hundreds of well-fed cats had gathered there in the cattery. Since they received their daily food without any effort, they did not move away from there except to relax and stroll.

A very charming example of such kind treatment of animals is that presented by a high-ranking Companion—Abū al-Dardā'. At the time of his death he said to his camel, "O my camel! Do not quarrel with me before our Lord and Cherisher, for I never made you work beyond your capacity." There was another Companion by the name of ʿAdī ibn Ḥātim who crushed the bread into fine powder for the ants and said, "These are our neighbors, therefore they have a right over us." The great Imām Abū Isḥāq al-Shīrāzī was one day going along with his friends when a dog confronted him. Its master tried to drive it away from his path, but the Imām prevented him from doing so, saying, "Do you not know that the roads are common between us humans and dogs."

One cannot fully appreciate the value of this most outstanding aspect of Islamic Civilization and its kind attitude concerning the treatment of animals unless one knows how these poor creatures were treated in olden times and during the Middle Ages. First of all, one does not find prescribed in the teachings of other nations instructions legislating kindness and mercy to animal. Thus there is no trace of any obligation upon the owner of the animal to feed it and look after it. Furthermore, one comes across an incredible situation which existed during the Middle Ages and continued even up to the nineteenth century, in which an animal was made liable for its own crime or that of its owner. In the field of obligations and responsibilities, animals were treated in the same manner as rational human beings! Judgments were passed against animals just as they were passed against men. The animals would be imprisoned, exiled and put to death just as criminals would be put to death.

The following articles are to be found within Jewish Law: "If a bull gores a man or a woman with its horns and he or she dies as a consequence of it, the bull must in that case be stoned to death.

His meat is prohibited for consumption and the owner of the bull will not be liable if the animal was not habitually aggressive. However, if it was habitual for the bull to be aggressive and the owner had also been warned that his animal was a potential danger, but did not even care to look after it properly and it thus caused someone's death, the offending animal would be stoned to death and the owner would also be put to death." There is another situation too where the animal is punished under Jewish Law. This is when a person is found guilty of bestiality; the person guilty of such an unnatural heinous crime and the animal, the object of this crime, both shall be put to death.

The ancient Greeks had an exclusive court to try and punish animals found guilty of the death of a man or a woman, so much so that even lifeless objects that were the cause of the death of a person were tried. This court was called "Berteoneon." Plato also wrote in his book of Laws that if an animal killed a person, the members of the family of the person killed had the right to sue the animal, and the guardians of the person killed were also entitled to select the judge from amongst the landlords. In case of the guilt being proved, the killing of that animal became obligatory, and the carcass was thrown outside the country. However, when it came to animals that were reared for combat against men on the occasion of festivals and sports, if a person was killed in combat against the animal, the latter was not considered guilty of murder. If an inanimate object fell on a person causing his death, the closest relative of the deceased was appointed the judge, who would give the decision of throwing the object beyond the bounds of the country. Animals were convicted not only in cases of loss of life, but for all other less serious crimes. For example, in the case of a dog biting a person, the owner of the dog was bound to bring that dog securely held with ropes and present it to the bitten person, who then had a right to take whatever revenge on it he pleased. He could kill it, inflict, corporal punishment on it or any other treatment that he deemed appropriate.

Similarly, animals were punished because of the crime of their owner or his family. The family, animals and slaves of any man who had been sentenced to death for crimes against the State would be burnt by fire, killed or banished.

One of the articles of the ancient Roman Law was that if a farmer's bull, during the period of cultivation, crossed its owner's field and went into the neighbor's field, the bull and its owner both were both put to death. The least punishment for a dog biting a person was that it was handed over to the person bitten so that he might do with it what he liked. Similarly, if an animal grazed on another person's bramble, it too was handed over to the master of the land. These Greek and Roman Laws relating to animals were also the norm in ancient Germany.

In ancient Persia, the laws relating to animals were even more barbaric. If a rabid dog bit a child and killed him, or in case of biting a man, wounded him, then the right ear of that dog would be cut off. If it had the audacity to repeat the offence, the left ear was chopped off. Repeating it for the third time would make it liable to lose its right leg and a fourth offence deprived it of the left leg also. And if it survived these amputations, and repeated the offence for the fifth time, its tail was removed completely.

During the Middle Ages, France was the first country among the European nation to make animals responsible for their actions and try them in a court, just as human beings were tried. The charges against them were brought under the same law that was used for men. At the close of the fourteenth century, Sardinia too adopted the same laws, and during the last part of the fifteenth century, Belgium enforced this law. In the middle of the sixteenth century, Holland, Germany, Italy and Sweden followed suit. In some parts of Sicily this law persisted up to the nineteenth century.

A case would be taken up against an animal either at the request of the person affected or at the request of the government. Advocates representing the accused animal appeared in court and tried to defend it. At times, the court sentenced the animal to a term of imprisonment as a precaution. The judgement would then be pronounced and executed in the presence of the public, as was the custom in the case of men. Sometimes the animal was stoned to death, beheaded or burnt, or had its limbs amputated or its organs removed before being killed. These cases were not brought against the animals for the sake of amusement or as mere consolation to the injured party. Rather, they were taken up in a very serious manner. The diction of the decisions and the legal orders indicate that they were very serious: "The animal is sentenced to death so that the demand of Justice may be met," or "It is crucified since it has been guilty of the most barbaric and heinous crimes."

The most barbaric traditions are those in which it has been said that people commenced proceedings against animals for meddling with the law of nature. Animals were charged with sorcery, which was such a crime, in their code of justice, that its perpetrator deserved nothing short of burning at the stake. On occasions of enforcing punishments on animals, ceremonial gatherings were held. The executioners came with logs of wood which were placed in the centre of an open ground. The cats convicted and sentenced were brought in iron cages. When it came to the execution, some monks visited the scene and held two burning brands to light the wood of the pyre. When it was lighted the officials ordered that the cats should be thrown into the flames so that they might be burnt to ashes, since they were guilty of crimes such as sorcery.

The comparisons between the attitude of the Islamic Civilization and those of others relating to animals have been clearly presented. It has clearly shown that the Muslim *Ummah* stands out among the ancient peoples and the modern nations in two things which are conspicuous by their absence elsewhere.

First, Muslims established collective instructions and made arrangements for the infirmity, old age and sickness of the animals. Second, Islam put a stop to animals being made accountable for their actions, credit for which modern civilization is seeking. That is why the history of the Islamic Civilization is totally free from the nonsensical cases brought up against dumb animals. Moreover, the Islamic Civilization strictly put an end to the cruel practice of animal combats—cock, ram and bullfights, whereas the Greeks and the Romans regarded it lawful and a source of great pleasure. Even today in Spain, the brutal sport of bullfighting is a lawful and favorite pastime.

CHAPTER LIGHT

WELFARE INSTITUTIONS

THERE IS NO greater indication of the progress and worthiness of a nation and its deserved right to the leadership of the world than through the elevation of human concern for its individuals—an elevation which shines with goodness, righteousness and mercy throughout all strata of society. This includes everything that lives on earth, from humans to animals. It is by these criteria that civilizations of different nations become unique and are singled out. The influence and traces left behind in this field are how the superiority of one civilization over another is judged.

The Muslim *Ummah* attained an elevation in this field that has not been surpassed by any other nation which preceded it nor by any nation that followed it until now. The nations of the past kept the ideas of virtue and goodness limited to the places of worship and the seats of learning.

The only motivation of the Muslim *Ummah* in doing good and pious work was to seek the pleasure of Allah, whether people knew about this or not. Evidence that substantiates this claim is that Ṣalāḥuddīn al-Ayyūbī spent all his wealth in public welfare works and filled the lands of Syria and Egypt with welfare institutions such as mosques, schools, lodgings for travellers and other such institutions. However, he never named any of those institutions after him. Instead, he titled them with the names of his military officers, ministers, helpers and friends.

Moreover, the Islamic Civilization established institutions based on such welfare and social solidarity which, even today, the Western nations have not created. It causes such amazement and awe and indicates that the philanthropic concept of the Muslim *Ummah* was more comprehensive, purer and more expansive in its horizons than the philanthropic concept of any other nation.

Before we begin to discuss the various forms of public welfare institution in the Islamic Civilization throughout the ages, it would be appropriate to explain the basic principles of the Islamic Civilization relating to public welfare. These principles had profound influence on the individuals of the Muslim *Ummah*. As a result these institutions came into existence and remain unparalleled in the history of mankind.

Islam calls for goodness in such a way that it defeats the human instincts of greed and the satanic whispers of fear of poverty. After encouraging the believers to have faith in the way of Allah, the Quran goes onto say, *Satan threatens you with poverty and bids you to conduct unseemly. Allah has promised you His Forgiveness and bounties* (Quran, 2:268).

Islam calls every capable person to goodness, whether he is rich or poor. If he is rich then he can do good with his wealth and his position of influence, and if he is poor, he can do good with his hand, his heart, his tongue and his deed. Under the Islamic order, there can be no person who cannot do good in one way or another.

You will not find a human who can't improve himself in the field of righteousness and goodness in Islam. Some of the poorer Companions of the Prophet ﷺ complained to him that the rich had surpassed them in doing good because they were able to donate their wealth, and as for the poor, they didn't have anything to donate. The Messenger ﷺ made it clear to them that giving wealth was not the only form of goodness. Rather, every benefit to people is considered a good action: "For every glorification [of Allah] is a *ṣadaqa* [charity], enjoining good is *ṣadaqa*, forbidding evil is *ṣadaqa*, removing obstacles from the path is *ṣadaqa*, to reconcile between two people is *ṣadaqa*, and to help a man onto his mount is also *ṣadaqa.*" (Bukhārī and Muslim).

In this way, Islam opens the doors of goodness to everyone from all walks of life. The blind, the infirm and the farmer can do good without their economic situation deterring them from spreading righteousness and goodness in society. Islam elevates the souls to the highest horizon of philanthropy where goodness is placed for all of the servants of Allah regardless of their faiths, their languages, their homelands and their race. The Prophet ﷺ said, "All of creation are the children of Allah. So the most beloved to Allah is he who is of utmost benefit to His children." (Ṭabarānī).

Islam addresses the human psyche so that goodness and righteousness are in one's interest because it benefits man himself. It addresses every human by saying that the good-doer shall be the first to benefit from it. He will benefit from the righteousness with reward, love [of the people], praise and eternity with Allah: *Whatever good you give benefits your own self* (Quran, 41:46); and *Whoever works righteousness benefits his own self* (Quran, 2:272).

If man is dominated by selfishness and loves himself before everything else then this approach has its affect on the human soul. However, in the shade of Islam, the miser becomes generous and the greedy gives from his wealth. He spends wealth on the people, and the thought of his children's needs does not prevent him from doing so.

Consider the following verse: *Who is he that will loan to Allah a beautiful loan, which Allah will double unto his credit and multiply many times?* (Quran, 2:245). When this verse was revealed, a Companion named Abū al-Daḥdaḥ asked the Prophet ﷺ, "O Messenger of Allah. Does Allah too ask His servants to give Him a loan?" The Prophet replied, "Yes." On this the Companion asked the Prophet to extend his hand and to bear witness that he had given away his garden that no one else owned, a garden in which there were seven hundred palm trees. The Companion returned to his garden where his wife and children were. He informed his wife of what he had done. The family vacated the garden, and she said to him, "What a profitable transaction, O Abū al-Daḥdaḥ!"

When the Quranic verse was revealed, *By no means shall you attain righteousness unless you give [freely] of that which you love* (Quran, 3:92), Abū Ṭalḥa al-Anṣārī said, "O Messenger of Allah! The most beloved of my wealth is Bayraha [a garden full of fruit-bearing trees] and it is a *ṣadaqa* for Allah. I hope for its righteousness and reward from Allah the Exalted. So take it, O Messenger of Allah, until Allah shows you [what to do with it]." The Prophet ﷺ said, "Excellent! That is profit. Keep it under your charge and give away the fruit."

This *ṣadaqa* was the first Islamic trust [*waqf*]—a system which financed all the social institutions in their noble humanitarian efforts. All the welfare institutions in the Islamic Civilization were essentially based on this system of *waqf*. In this regard, the Messenger of Allah was the best of examples for his *Ummah*. He gave away seven gardens as a trust as some *mujāhid* had made out a will that the Prophet ﷺ could do with them what he liked. The Prophet gave it as a trust for the poor, for those fighting for the cause of Allah and for those in need. ʿUmar ibn al-Khaṭṭāb endowed his land in Khaybar. Abū Bakr, ʿUthmān, ʿAlī, Zubayr and many others endowed their properties as trusts until there remained no Companion who had not given something away from his wealth as a trust.

This humanitarian work was once again revived during the rule of ʿUmar ibn al-Khaṭṭāb when he gave away as a trust a piece of land in the way of Allah. He called on a group of Anṣār and Muhājirūn and made them bear witness to that action. Jābir ibn ʿAbdullāh al-Anṣārī said, "I don't know of anyone from the Companions of the Messenger of Allah from among the Anṣār and the Muhājir except that he had given away as a trust some of his wealth." A charity which is a trust cannot be sold, or inherited or gifted. Muslims continued this practice of endowment, generation after generation, and lands, gardens, houses and the produce of the fields were given away as trusts. The Islamic

Society was so full of such institutions that it would be difficult to count them. These institutions comprise two types; the first being the expansive endowments of the State, and the second being those established by individuals. Although it is not possible for us to mention all the different types of welfare institutions here, it will suffice to mention the following:

1. The primary public welfare institution is the mosque. People competed with one another in building mosques to seek the pleasure of Allah. Even the kings competed with each other in building grand mosques. Walīd ibn ʿAbd al-Mālik spent such a big fortune on the construction of the Umayyad Mosque, and such a large number of men participated in its construction that the facts and figures appear almost incredible at first sight.

2. Construction of welfare institutions such as schools and hospitals.

3. Construction of inns and hotels for the travellers left behind when their caravans left. Poor people could also seek shelter in these guest houses.

4. Abodes for recluses and for those devoted entirely to the worship of Allah.

5. Building homes for the poor who could neither build nor rent homes for themselves.

6. A regular supply of drinking water on the streets.

7. Building restaurants where bread, meat, soup and a sweet dish were provided. Even today, one finds such places as the Takya Sultan Salīm and Takya Shaykh Muḥiyuddīn in Damascus.

8. Building houses for the Hajj pilgrims in Makkah where

they could stay for the duration of the Hajj. These houses were built in such large numbers that they had covered almost the entire land of Makkah. That is why some jurists issued verdicts against letting out houses in Makkah since, in their opinion, all the houses in Makkah were originally meant as trusts for the Hajj pilgrims.

9. Digging wells in ravines and mountain valleys so that they may serve cattle, agricultural needs and travellers. There were many such wells between Baghdad and Makkah, between Damascus and Madina and between other capitals, cities and villages of the Islamic State.

10. Building posts for frontier guards facing the danger of potential foreign attack on the country. There were several such institutions exclusively meant for frontier guards where they would have everything they required ranging from weapons and ammunitions to food and drink. It was due to the establishment of such institutions that during the period of the ʿAbbāsids an attack by the Romans was prevented. Similarly, the Crusades of the Western countries against Syria and Egypt also came to an end.

11. Trusts for the provisions of horses, swords, spears and other weapons of war, which provided the Mujāhidīn with all the required military hardware. This had the effect of promoting the war industries in Muslim countries to a considerable degree, and large factories of arms production were established in their cities. Even the Crusaders went freely to Muslim lands, during the period of truce, to purchase weapons from the Muslims. The scholars of the time issued verdicts prohibiting the sales of arms

to the enemy. How different things have become today! Muslims have to beg the Western countries for arms, which they do not offer except with conditions that damage the self-respect and independence of Muslims.

12. Trusts whose income was meant exclusively for those venturing out to fight in the way of Allah [*Jihād*] and for those men engaged in fighting when the State could not meet the expenses of every individual. If Muslims did this today, it would result in the establishment of factories, equipping the Muslim army with weapons and ammunitions necessary to prevent aggression and protect its lands.

13. Trusts whose income was meant for the construction and repair of roads, pathways and bridges.

14. Trust of lands to serve as burial grounds; people endowed large tracts of lands to be used as general graveyards.

15. Trusts for the burial of the deceased who are poor and everything associated with it.

16. In spite of the abundance of trusts for social support, there were exclusive trusts for children and orphans who had no support.

17. Institutions for the disabled, blind and helpless, where all their necessities like food, clothes, shelter, education and training were provided and where they could spend a life of honor and dignity.

18. Institutions for improving the condition of prisoners, raising their standard of living, providing them with food and protecting their health.

19. Institutions whose income was to be spent on those

looking after the blind and the disabled.

20. Trusts to look after the marriage of young men and women whose guardians could not pay for their expenses like the *mahr* [dowry]. How compassionate to think of such people and how much Muslims stand in need of this sentiment today!

21. Institutions established to help mothers, supplying them with milk and sugar. Such institutions were established on the basis of seeking the pleasure of Allah the Exalted. One of the philanthropic deeds of Ṣalāḥuddīn al-Ayyūbī was to establish two reservoirs, one of milk and the other of fresh drinking water close to the gate of his fort, which still stands in Damascus today. Twice a week, mothers of young babies and children would come and take milk and sugar for the needs of their children.

22. Welfare institutions, astonishing as it may seem, which replaced broken bowls of those children who accidentally broke theirs in transit from the market to their homes. Visiting these institutions, they would take a new bowl and return to their families as though nothing happened.

23. Institutions and trusts established for the treatment of sick animals, to feed them and provide pastures for permanently disabled animals. The area of *Marj al-Akhḍar* in Damascus, where the municipal stadium stands today, was one such trust. It was a trust for the horses and discarded aged animals pasturing therein until the end of their lives.

These institutions established for public welfare in the Islamic Civilization fell more or less into thirty categories. Can one find any equivalent in any other nation? In fact, there is no counterpart for many of them in contemporary Western civilization. Allah is our witness that this was the path of life along which we trod alone while the rest of the world was wandering aimlessly in a state of unawareness, ignorance, backwardness and darkness. By Allah! This is the path of eternal life which rid civilization of humanity's grief and misery.

Alas! Which path have Muslims taken today? Where are those hands that wiped and dried the tears of the orphans, comforted the wounded hearts and made the Muslim society one in which everyone was united and all lived happily in security, goodness, honor and peace?

CHAPTER NINE

SCHOOLS AND EDUCATIONAL INSTITUTIONS

ISLAMIC SCHOOLS WERE established with the income of large properties from Muslim endowments. Different noblemen, leaders, scholars, traders and ruler had instituted these trusts at different times. These schools were so numerous that there was hardly any town or village that went without one, and within them many teachers were employed for public instruction.

In the Islamic Civilization, the mosque was the centre which developed the school. At that time, the mosque was not only a place of worship; its extensive open space served as a school where young children learned how to read and write and learned the Quran, *Sharīʿah*, Grammar and branches of various other disciplines. Next to the mosques *kuttāb* were established that specifically taught reading, writing, Arabic and Mathematics. These *kuttāb* resembled the present day primary schools; and there were so many that Ibn Hawqal calculated that there were three hundred *kuttāb* in one of the towns of Sicily. They were so spacious that at any one time hundreds and thousands of students could be taught. Abū al-Qāsim al-Balkhī writes about his own *kuttāb* in which three thousand students would learn, "Its compound was so wide that a donkey had to be used [to go from one part to the other] for the supervision of the students."

Then came the establishment of schools next to the mosques and *kuttāb*. Such schools resembled the secondary and high schools of today. The education provided was free of charge for all classes. The students did not pay any fees as they do now and it was not restricted to certain groups and social classes at the expense of others. The opportunity for education was available to everybody. So the son of the rich would sit next to the son of the poor, the son of the trader would sit next to the son of the worker or the farmer.

The education in the schools were of two types: an internal section for the poor who could not financially afford to live on the wealth of their parents and an external section for those who wanted to return to their families in the evening. The internal section [boarding] was also free and provided food and a bed for the student. Every school had a mosque, classrooms, residential quarters for the students, library, kitchen and toilet facilities. Some schools also had playgrounds outside. Even today there are examples of these types of schools which were previously to be found throughout the entire Islamic world. In Damascus, there is still al-Madrasah al-Nūriyyah founded by the great hero Nūruddīn al-Shahīd. It stands in the "Market of the Weavers" and is still operating and providing us with the mechanics of the schools established during Islamic Civilization. Ibn Jubayr, the traveller, visited it in the beginning of the seventh century after *hijrah*. He was so impressed with it that he wrote, "From among the best schools in the world is the school of Nūruddīn, may Allah have mercy on him. It is one of the most elegant palaces ever established. For its water supply, a canal has been constructed up to the school building, in the centre of which stands a fountain, dividing the falling water into two small streams which further on join to fill a big reservoir situated in the centre of this palace. The beauty of the scene is captivating."

In spite of the fact that the vicissitudes of life have played havoc with this institution and several segments of it have been snatched away, its building, classrooms, the mosque, the residential quarters of the teachers and their retiring rooms have survived. These retiring rooms served the purpose of the staff-rooms of the modern schools and colleges. A special house too stands there which was the residence of the head master or principal of the school with his family. The residences of the students and the servants of the school also stand to this day. Presently the neighbors of this school have taken possession of the school-kitchen, the spacious dining hall and the kitchen store for the storage of grains, vegetables and other food materials. This building of the school is a living pattern of the Muslim schools of olden days.

Similarly the Qawmī, Shāhī and ʿUthmānī schools of Aleppo stand as monuments to past glory, where the students' hostel rooms and classrooms are still standing today. Earlier these schools provided catering for their students. Later on, however, the students paid their own expenses, including those for food, at the end of every month.

The mosque of al-Azhar is also a living specimen of a school within a mosque, wherein students gather to pursue their studies under the guidance of a teacher in various different sections. Around the mosque are rooms known as *warrāq* where these students reside and live in their own groups. For example, there were separate *warrāq* for the Syrian, Turkish, Sudanese and Iraqi students. Even today, the students of al-Azhar University get monthly stipends along with their free education from the income of the properties endowed for al-Azhar.

The principals of these schools used to come from among the best and most famous of scholars. The biographies of the famous scholars mention the schools that they taught in. Imām al-Nawawī, Ibn al-Ṣalāḥ, Abū Shamma, Taqīyuddīn Subkī and ʿImāduddīn ibn Kathīr taught at the "House of Hadith" in Damascus. Ghazālī, Shirāzī, Imām al-Ḥaramayn, ʿAllāma Shāsī, Khaṭīb al-Tabrīzī, Qazwinī and Fayrūzabādī and others taught at the Madrasah Niẓāmiyyah in Baghdad. In the early period, these teachers never accepted any remuneration for their services. However, at the height of Islamic Civilization, great seats of learning came into existence, large endowments were made for them and resulted in monthly salaries which were allocated in the budgets for the teachers.

It would be interesting to mention here, the incident regarding the insight and far-sightedness of the scholars of Mawara al-Nahr. When Niẓām al-Mulk instituted his famous schools in the cities and fixed monthly salaries were allocated to the teachers, the scholars gathered together and objected to this move and mourned over the intended change that, according to them, was the commercialization of a noble profession and would take away the value and blessings of knowledge. Knowledge, in their opinion, should be taught solely for its nobility and grandeur so as to attain perfection in learning. Now that material gain was to be attached to learning, those avaricious for material benefits and personal interest would throng to the centres of learning with the result that knowledge and learning themselves would no longer be of value, but rather become poor in quality and suffer degradation. In consideration of the changing times and the growing needs of the society, however, this point of view was not accepted. So finally the salaries of the teachers were allocated. These differed from place to place in keeping with the various regions, the status of the school and the endowments supporting it. Still these salaries were adequate for a decent living for the teachers. In addition to remuneration for teaching, they were paid subsistence allowance for their economic needs. Shaykh Najmuddīn Habushānī, who had been appointed the principal of Madrasah Ṣalāḥiyyah by Sultan Ṣalāḥuddīn, was paid forty pounds for his services of teaching, ten pounds for the supervision of the trusts of the school, and a daily ration of sixty Egyptian Ratals of bread and two leather bags full of water from the Nile. The Shaykh of al-Azhar had his allowance also, charged to the particular endowment of al-Azhar to which he charged the maintenance of his horse. This amounted to about a hundred pounds in later periods and was finally merged with the salary of Shaykh al-Azhar.

Only those people who were certified by the experts as being perfectly fit for the job were allowed to teach. During the early days of Islam, the teachers themselves permitted their bright and capable students to detach themselves from the teacher and start their own circles of teaching. Or in case of the death of the teacher, the brightest student of his circle was elected to take the seat of the teacher. If anyone did otherwise, then he would be the subject of much criticism.

Abū Yūsuf, the Chief Justice during the rule of Hārūn al-Rashīd, fell seriously ill during the lifetime of his teacher, Imām Abū Ḥanīfah. The teacher came to ask about the health of his favorite pupil and said that he was very much worried about his illness. Abū Ḥanīfah told him that he expected Abū Yūsuf to succeed him in serving the needs of the Muslims. Abū Yūsuf got over that illness and became impressed with himself at the remarks of his teacher. He decided to start his own circles independent of the circles of Imām Abū Ḥanīfah. Abū Ḥanīfah sent someone to him with five questions which required clear explanatory answers. Abū Yūsuf made errors in answering them, realized the mistake of leaving his teacher and thus returned to his circles. Abū Ḥanīfah said to him, "You were like a dried fruit before it was ripe. The one who thinks that he does no need to learn should cry for himself."

Such was the culture in the early period of the development of the educational system. However, when schools were well established, they started awarding academic certificates which would be given by the Shaykh of the school. These certificates resemble the degrees, diplomas and certificates of present times. The physicians, in particular, were not allowed to establish their practice until they had formally obtained a certificate [of competence] from the physicians of the school.

The teachers used to put on a particular type of dress which distinguished them from other professions. The dress at the time of Abū Yūsuf was a black turban and a sheet. During the Fatimid dynasty it was a green turban, a golden dress comprising six pieces, with a cap and a sheet. The gown, which was exclusive to the scholars and the teachers, had come in to use during the period of the Umayyid rule. In Andalusia, the dress of the teachers and the scholars was slightly different from the dress of the scholars of the East. The more marked difference lay in the turban which was very small in their case. Some even went without a turban. So when Imām Abū ʿAlī al-Qalī, the famous linguist, visited Andalusia, the local scholars came to greet him and they were surprised at his big turban. The dim-witted people and children even made fun of him and threw pebbles at him. The graduation gowns and caps now known in the European universities have their origin in the dress of the teachers of Andalusia.

Teachers had their own independent union, like the union of students, union of nobles and union of different types of workmen. The teachers elected their president and they were totally independent in this matter. The State interfered in these matters only when any dissension arose among them.

Abū Shamah reported in his *Rawḍatayn* that when Ḥāfiẓ Murādī died, there were two groups among the jurists: Arab and Kurd. Some of them were inclined towards *Fiqh* and therefore wanted Shaykh Sharfuddīn ibn Abī Asrun to fill the vacancy. However, others had an inclination for logical sciences and ethics, and were in favor of al-Quṭub al-Nīsapūrī. Thus there was dissension between the scholars on this matter. Nūruddīn got to hear of it and invited the group of scholars to see him. He deputized Majduddīn ibn Dayah to speak to them on his behalf. He said to them, "We did not intend the construction of schools except for the spread of knowledge and eradication of innovation. That which is taking place among yourselves is not good and is not befitting." Nūruddīn said, "Let us please both parties and invite both of the scholars." Sharfuddīn was placed in charge of the school named after him and al-Quṭub was placed in charge of the school of Nafrī.

The Islamic world was characterized by an abundance of schools and institutions of higher education. Islamic history prides itself on being able to present the names of such sons of Islam who played an important role in building big schools in every city of the Islamic world. The name of Ṣalāḥuddīn al-Ayyūbī tops the list. He had established a network of schools in every part of Egypt, Damascus, Mosul, and Bayt al-Maqdis. Nūruddīn, the martyr, is also among those people. He established fourteen big schools in Syria alone, out of which six were established in Damascus, four in Aleppo, two in Ḥama and Ḥums and one in Baᶜlbak. Niẓām al-Mulk Ṭūṣī, the Chief Minister of the Suljūqs is also one of those men. He had filled Iraq and Khurasān with schools. The historians mention that he established an educational institution for higher studies in every city of Iraq and Khurasān and founded schools in places far off from the principal cities and towns. For example, he established a magnificent school in Jazīra ibn ᶜUmar which was very beautiful and imposing. Wherever he heard of a learned man of extraordinary worth, he instituted a school for him there with adequate endowments to support and maintain it. A large library was also established for the benefit of the school.

Niẓāmiyyah of Baghdad was the most important and well organized educational institution. Between the fifth and ninth century of the *hijrah*, great learned men graduated from this institution. The students on its register reached six thousand and among them were the children of the rich and the indigent, studying side by side, neither of them paying any educational fees. However, for the poor students, in addition to free education, there were stipends to meet all their needs, paid to them from the income of lands endowed for this purpose.

Along with these great men of high rank and position, there were other wealthy people and traders who also competed with one another in establishing schools and arranging endowments for their support and maintenance so that with these endowments the school could be financed. There have also been many other generous people who had converted their own houses into schools and whatever collection of books they had or the properties in their possession were endowed for the benefit of the students.

For these reasons, the Madrasas were in great abundance in the entire Islamic world in general and in the Eastern Muslim countries in particular. Ibn Jubayr, the well known traveller of Andalusia, was amazed to see the abundance of these Madrasas, their endowments, the plentiful food production and unlimited income, which had induced the people of Andalusia to go East to acquire knowledge. He says, "In the Eastern countries there are countless endowments for the students of the Madrasas, particularly in Damascus. The Western [Andalusian] students who desire security, ease and affluence should go there. There, they find many advantages which will be helpful to them in their quest for knowledge and particularly in economic matters, with the result that they will be free from care and anxiety."

Ibn Jubayr's confirmation has special significance, for he enjoys a position as a reliable and honest traveller when it comes to the presentation of facts. He made particular mention of Damascus with regard to the abundance of trusts and the number of Madrasas. At that time there were more than four hundred fully functioning Madrasas in the city, with students coming to them from far off places. In this regard, the historical evidence is also of great interest, stating that the abundance of Madrasas in Damascus made it impossible for a student coming to this town for one year's sojourn to stay more than one night at any one of these schools, and thus his sojourn came to an end.

In his history, Ibn ᶜAsākir has quoted a eulogy of Sultan Ibn ᶜAlī ibn Manqaz al-Katanī exalting Damascus. In this poem he has mentioned the Madrasas of Damascus in these words, "There you will find such teachers, to whom you may present any problem and then let some young man come forward to solve it for you immediately. Whoever goes there will be amazed and guided towards the right path. One who is poor in thought will become rich at once. With the produce of the trust properties of these schools, the prisoners obtain their release and the poor become rich and contented. There are imāms [authorities in learning] who impart knowledge and there are such masters of the system of self-purification who can provide a cure for all the ills of the psyche, although these ills are very complicated."

Now we shall put forth some examples which gives an idea of the abundance of endowments. The endowments of Madrasah Nūriyyah Kubra according to the document at its entrance, were the following, "All the new Turkish baths of the wheat market, two new baths of Wariqa outside Bāb al-Salām and their annex, the factory of Auniyah Hima and the small grove of Aq and Wazir, three fourth of the Jawza grove of Arza, the eleven shops outside Bāb Jabiyyah and nine fields of Dariyah."

The endowments for the Nūrī Hospital of Aleppo were as follows: "The entire village of Mi'rata, half of the cultivated land of the Aṣl valley of Saman mountain, five fiddān, land enough to be conveniently tilled by five pairs of oxen from the land of Kufr Tanān, one third of the Khālidī field, a flour mill of Malakh, as also the entire income of the flour mill in front of Bāb al-Khubbān, three fiddān from the field of Abū Miraya, eight pairs of oxen worth of land from the Khumayr field of Matakh, land worth eleven pairs of oxen from the Farzal field of Mu'arrah, one third of the income of Bayt Rayl village of Ghazbiyat, ten shops of Hawa market, the general stores and shops outside Bāb Intakiyyah, Bāb Marah and Bāb Jinān."

To give an idea of the abundance of endowments for the mosques and Madrasas of Damascus, it would suffice to mention that Imām Nawawī (d. 676 AH) never tasted a fruit grown in Damascus all his life, since the greater part of the gardens of

Damascus were endowed properties which had been misappropriated by tyrants.

There were many schools meant for various purposes. Some of them imparted knowledge of the Quran only, such as its commentary, recital and commitment to memory. There were others that taught hadith and relevant disciplines. There were many others exclusively imparting knowledge of *Fiqh*. Again, there was a separate Madrasah for every school of *Fiqh*. Similarly, there were separate Madrasas for the education of medicine and there were also schools only for the orphans.

Naʿīmī, who was the most outstanding among the scholars of the tenth century, has given a complete list of the schools of Damascus and their endowments in his book *al-Daramīn fī'l-Tārīkh al-Madāris*. It tells us that there were seven Madrasas meant exclusively for the education of the Quran and relevant disciplines, sixteen for the teaching of hadith, three for the Quran and hadith combined, sixty-three Madrasas for Shāfiʿī *Fiqh*, fifty-two for Ḥanafī *Fiqh*, four for the Mālikī school of *Fiqh* and eleven for Ḥanbalī *Fiqh*. There were entirely separate schools for the education of medical sciences. There were also more houses of retreat, inns and the great congregation mosques than schools. It must be remembered that in all these places there was pursuit of teaching and learning in full swing.

Comparing these conditions with those prevailing in the West at the time would be advisable. One may be surprised to learn that they were totally ignorant and ill-mannered. Knowledge was confined to the monasteries of the monks and hermits, and was exclusive to the soothsayers and priests. From this comparison, it becomes obvious what heights the Muslim *Ummah* had reached. From the point of view of the history of social institutions and centres of learning, the feats of Islamic Civilization are magnificent. It is amazing that Islam spared no pains in the propagation of knowledge, in raising the standard of human civilization and providing these facilities for all the individuals of every religion and community.

Ibn Kathīr, in his book *al-Bidāya wa al-Nihāya*, writes under the events of 631 AH, "This year the building of Madrasah Mustanṣariyyah was completed. No such Madrasah was ever built before that. This was dedicated to all the four schools of *Fiqh*. Sixty-two jurists of every school of *Fiqh* worked at this Madrasah. Four of them were experts, one a teacher of every school, one a Shaykh of hadith, two reciters well versed in the recital of the Quran with proper intonation, ten careful listeners who guarded against the reciter making any lapses and correcting him on the spot, one a Shaykh of Medicine and ten Muslim physicians who ran the clinics. There was also a *maktab* of orphans. For every student there was a fixed quantity of bread, meat and sweets and a particular amount of money for other expenses which was far in excess of their needs."

He goes on further to say, "For the school, a library was endowed, which was unparalleled in our knowledge. There were a large number of books and some of the best specimens of the art of calligraphy. The best books of every discipline were collected here."

CHAPTER TEN

HOSPITALS AND MEDICAL INSTITUTIONS

ONE OF THE principles that Islamic Civilization is based upon is that both the physical and spiritual needs of man have been safeguarded. Islamic Civilization paid due attention to the development and care of the physique so that along with a resplendent soul, man may attain the highest position in development. In this connection, the words of the founder of Islamic Civilization, Prophet Muḥammad ﷺ, are worthy of attention, "Assuredly the body too has a claim over you" (Bukhārī and Muslim). ʿAlī ibn ʿAbbās has defined medicine as "the science which investigates the preservation of health and returning health to the ill."

If all the forms of Islamic worship are carefully examined, principles of public health and hygiene, which are the most important objective of medical science, have been kept in view, with attention drawn to the minutest details. So it is observed that all the conditions laid down for prayer, fasting and Hajj, and in whatever manner the body has to exert itself during their performance, are extremely useful for its hygiene, maintaining health and keeping the body fresh and active. Furthermore, the Islamic Civilization combated the spread of diseases, and people have been encouraged to accept treatment for every disease. The field of medicine has been founded upon strong principles and its feats have attained great heights in this field. It established large hospitals and other medical institutions which benefited the entire humanity. This institution produced such medical men of extraordinary standards, of whose accomplishments in the field of learning and technical work, the world is indebted to this day.

The Arabs were acquainted with the Medical College at Chandesapu, established by the emperor of Persia in the latter half of the sixth century of the Christian Era. Some of the Arab physicians had also been trained at this Medical College. For example, Ḥārith ibn Kaldah who lived during the time of the Prophet ﷺ, was the medical advisor to some of the Companions, looking after them when they fell ill.

Muslims established their first ever hospital during the period of Walīd ibn ʿAbd al-Mālik, which was meant exclusively for leprosy patients. The physicians appointed to this hospital were granted large properties and salaries. Those undergoing treatment had orders to stay at the hospitals permanently and were granted stipends, just as they had been granted to the blind. Thereafter a whole series of hospitals and asylums for the infirm were built.

Hospitals were of two kinds—mobile dispensaries and permanent buildings. One such mobile dispensary is traceable to the period of the Prophet ﷺ and was established during the Battle of the Trench. In this battle, a separate tent was erected for the wounded. When Saʿd ibn Muʿādh was wounded and one of the blood vessels of his arm was injured, the Prophet ﷺ ordered that he should be kept in the tent for the wounded so that he might personally look after him. This was the first mobile military dispensary in Islam. Later on, the Caliphs and the rulers developed and extended them to the extent that all the requirements of patients ranging from medical care, diet, medicines, clothes, physicians and pharmacists were provided. These mobile hospitals moved from village to village where there were no permanent hospitals.

ʿAlī ibn ʿĪsā ibn al-Jarrāḥ wrote to Sinān ibn Thābit who was then in charge of the hospitals in and around Baghdad, and those affiliated to it, "I have been thinking of the people living in the village of Ṣawad where they have been falling sick but failed to receive medical attention due to the lack of physicians. Could you bring together a group of physicians and provide them with a fairly large stock of medicines and antidotes for their use? They should go to the villages and stay as long as it may be necessary, and after they have treated all the patients there, they should move on to another village."

During the reign of Sultan Muḥammad Saljūqī, the mobile hospital had become so large that forty camels carried its equipment. As for the permanent hospitals, they were in such large numbers that every big and small town benefited from them. Even the smallest town boasted of more than one hospital. For example, Cordoba alone had fifty major hospitals.

The nature of these hospitals had changed too. Some of them were reserved for the army personnel and had their own special physicians. These physicians were in addition to the special physicians attending to the Caliphs, the military commanders, and the nobles. There were separate hospitals for the prisoners. The physician examined the prisoners everyday and they were provided with the necessary facilities of treatment.

ʿAlī ibn ʿĪsā ibn al-Jarrāḥ once wrote to the Chief Medical Officer of Baghdad, "I am very much worried about the prisoners. Their large numbers and conditions makes it certain that there must be many ailing persons among them. Therefore, I am of the opinion that they must have their own physicians who should examine them everyday and give them, when necessary, medicines and antidotes. Such physicians should visit all prisons and treat the sick prisoners there."

There were also first aid centres which were usually located at busy public places such as mosques with a large congregation. Maqrizī writes, "When Ibn Tulūn built his world famous mosque in Egypt, at one end there was a place for ablution and a dispensary. The dispensary was well equipped with medicines and attendants. On Fridays, there used to be a standby physician who used to aid and assist any emergencies."

Some hospitals were of a general nature, open to all at all hours of the day and night. They were of two types—male-only hospitals and female-only hospitals. Each type of hospital had several departments dealing with different diseases: systemic diseases, ophthalmology, surgery, orthopedics and psychology. The department of systemic diseases was further divided into sub-sections dealing with fevers and digestive troubles.

Every department had an officer-in-charge and a presiding

officer, as well as a specialist of its own. There was also a superintendent, supervising the work and management of the entire institution. There were fixed working hours for the physicians during which they attended to the patients coming to their departments.

Every hospital had its own junior staff of pharmacists and nurses. Their salaries were fixed and were reasonably lucrative. Every hospital had a pharmacy known as the "Store of Medications," which comprised many kinds of fluid medicines, fine electuaries and high quality medicinally preserved fruit. Moreover, there were some very refined preparations and juices, essences and distilled decoctions, available only at the hospitals and nowhere else. They also had fine surgical instruments, glass containers and other vessels which previously were to be found only in the palaces of the kings.

These hospitals served as institutions for the training of medical students, and every hospital had a large lecture theatre where the Chief Medical Officer, other physicians and medical students used to gather. All kinds of medical books and surgical instruments were available. After the patients had been attended to, the students used to sit before the teachers and discuss medical problems. These discussions were of practical importance and very useful. The textbooks were of a high standard. Often the teachers took their students with them to the hospital wards where they participated in the practical work, just as present day students are given the opportunity to see patients and practical work in the hospitals attached to the medical colleges. Ibn Abī Uṣaybaᶜa, who studied medicine at the Nūrī Hospital of

Damascus, writes, "When Ḥakīm Muhazabuddīn and Ḥakīm ʿImrān finished their examination and treatment of patients in the hospitals, I would be with them and sit with Shaykh Raḍiyuddīn Rahabī. I would observe their methodology and arguments in arriving at the diagnosis of diseases. Whatever statements they made about the patients and whatever they prescribed for them, I discussed with them most of those diseases and their prescriptions."

No physician was allowed to practice on his own. Anyone who wished to establish a practice had to appear before the Chief Medical Officer appointed by the government to prove his worth. He had to write a treatise on the subject in which he wanted to obtain a certificate of proficiency. This treatise was either his own writing or somebody else's, in which case he had to write his notes and comments. The Chief Medical Officer would interview him at length and question him on all the relevant topics of his subject. If he succeeded in giving satisfactory answers, he would permit the candidate to practice.

In the period of Muqtadir Billah (319 AH), some physicians treated a patient incorrectly, culminating in the patient's death. The Caliph ordered that all the physicians be re-examined. Thus the Chief Medical Officer, Sinān ibn Thābit, tested the capabilities of all the physicians. The number of physicians found and examined were more than 860. This excluded those who were not examined from among the well-known physicians and those who treated the Caliph, ministers and the nobility.

It should also be kept in mind that every large hospital had a library for the benefit of both the students and the physicians. It is said that the Ibn Tulūn Hospital of Egypt had a library comprising 100,000 books on various branches of medical science.

The portals of these hospitals were open to everybody and no fees of any kind were charged. No distinction was made between the poor and the rich, related and the stranger, local and foreign, common man and distinguished person. In the outpatient department, the patients were carefully examined and in the case of those in need of casual attention they were given the prescribed medicines to be taken at home. However, those who had serious conditions requiring regular attention and supervision were registered as inpatients. The patient would be sent to the changing room and would be provided with a clean hospital uniform, while the patient's own clothes were kept in the hospital store. The patient would then be taken to the hospital ward where a bed was ready for him or her with clean sheets. The course of the treatment prescribed by the doctor would immediately start. The patient would be given a nourishing diet to aid his recovery and improve his or her health. The quality of diet was also fixed and the patient would receive mutton, beef, meat of poultry and and other birds. The patient who was cured of his malady but remained weak would be transferred to the ward for convalescents until he or she was fully cured. Before discharge, the patient was given a new dress and enough monetary aid to establish a means of livelihood. The hospital rooms and wards were neat and tidy, with a regular supply of water and furnished with clean carpets. Every hospital had a sanitary inspector, accountants and other executive staff. The Caliph in office would visit these hospitals, meet the patients and take interest in their problems.

This was the excellent system at work in all the hospitals of the Islamic world, be they in the East or the West—this was the uniform system in all the hospitals of Baghdad, Damascus, Cairo, Bayt al-Maqdis, Makkah, Madinah and Andalusia. What follows is a description of the conditions of four major hospitals in four big cities of the Islamic world.

1. Azdi Hospital of Baghdad

Built by Azd al-Dawlah ibn Buwayh in 371 AH, the site for this hospital was selected by the then renowned physician, al-Rāzī [known as Rhazes of Europe]. He ordered that a piece of fresh meat be placed at night at each proposed site. Upon examination in the morning, the place where the meat was found least affected by degenerative changes was considered most suitable for the hospital and construction was thus undertaken. A magnificent building was constructed at a tremendous cost and twenty-four of the most capable physicians were selected for the staff. A library, pharmacy, store and kitchen were provided for the hospital, of which were well equipped. In 449 AH, the Caliph Qā'im bin Amrillāh renovated the hospital and equipped it with liquid medicines [infusions, decoctions, distilled extracts and syrups], herbs, roots and other medicines, which were of a rare nature. The patients were provided with sheets and blankets. Moreover, arrangements were made for perfumes, ice, attendants, postmen, sentinels, watchmen and physicians to be available all the time. A big complex of washing facilities with a supply of hot and cold water was constructed and a garden and orchard were provided with flowers and fruits of all kinds. The patients who were too weak to move and did not have access to any other conveyance were regularly transferred from various places to this hospital, and the physicians attended to them morning and evening during their hours of duty.

2. Nuri Hospital of Damascus

Sultan Mālik Nūruddīn, the martyr (549 AH), constructed this hospital with the ransom paid to him by one of the Christian monarchs. At the time of its construction this was the most beautiful hospital in the Islamic world. It was constructed specifically for the poor and helpless, and only in extenuating circumstances were the rich allowed to seek its aid. Ibn Jubayr visited the hospital in 580 AH. He praised the kind treatment delivered by the physicians and their devotional care in the preparation and administration of medicine and food for their patients. There was a special department set aside for the management of psychological cases. Individuals who were found to be dangerous had to be restrained for the safety of others. However, they were properly fed and looked after in the matter of treatment. The historians narrate that in 831 AH, a non-Arab visitor went to Damascus. He was not only a great learned person but had fine tastes too. He happened to visit the hospital and was amazed to see the wholehearted commitment and devotion of the physicians, as well as the service of food, hygiene and other facilities provided for patients. What was still more surprising was that over and above the normal amenities, the patients had decoration and luxury articles supplied to them. In order to test the skills of the physicians of that hospital he pretended to be ill and managed to get hospitalised for diagnosis and treatment. For three days the Chief Medical Officer noted his pulse and appeared to be diagnosing his trouble. However, he discovered the very first day that the "patient" was fit and healthy and had come only to test their skills. Therefore, he prescribed for him a rich diet of good poultry meat, sweet dishes, refreshing and stimulating drinks and various kinds of fruits. For three days he was given this diet at the hospital. After that, the Chief Medical Officer left a note for him which read, "Hospitality here is for a limited period of three days." That suggested to the non-Arab visitor that they had seen through his ruse and had entertained him only as a guest.

This hospital was functioning up until 1317 AH when it was converted to a hospital for foreigners. It is the same hospital which the Faculty of Medicine at the University of Syria now supervises. The Nūrī Hospital was thus shut down and a local school was established.

3. The Major Manṣūrī Hospital

This hospital used to be the palace of some members of the nobility. Mālik Manṣūr Sayfuddīn Qalaᶜūn converted it into a hospital in 683 AH and endowed a particular estate for it with an annual income of one-thousand dirhams. A mosque, a Madrasah and a maktab for the orphans were also established along with it. According to historians, the hospital was established when, in 1675 AD during the time of Zāhir Babyrus, the General set to oppose the advancing Roman armies, Amīr Qalaᶜūn, was suddenly taken ill at Damascus. The physicians treated him there and the medicines were supplied from the Nūrī Hospital. When he was completely cured he personally visited and inspected the Nūrī Hospital. He was very much impressed by it and vowed that if Allah brought him to rule, he would build a hospital like it. When he became the Sultan, he selected and purchased the palace and he converted it into a hospital. This hospital from the point of view of organization and disposition was the only hospital of its kind. Admittance and treatment was open to all. The patients discharged and cured from this hospital were given new clothes to wear and those who died were buried at the hospital's cost. There were separate physicians in charge of each branch of the medical sciences. There were attendants and nurses who washed the clothes of the patients, helped them to bathe, and cleaned and tidied the rooms and bedding. There were two attendees for every patient who did everything for their convenience and comfort. Every patient had a separate bed and bedding, and there were separate wards for patients of a certain type. There were fixed locations for discussions on medical themes and for lectures, where the principal used to teach the students. One of the unique aspects of this hospital was that treatment was not restricted only to inpatients, but was also provided for those who came as outpatients. They were supplied with medicines and nourishing food even under these conditions. Such was the extent of continuous medical treatment that one of the ophthalmologists at this hospital was reported to have said that more than four-thousand cases were treated daily. Those cured and discharged were offered clothes and cash to help them start some small business for their subsistence so that they would not be forced into difficult work immediately after coming out of hospital.

The documents relating to the endowments of these hospitals tell us that a patient in the hospital was given his food in a vessel reserved for his exclusive use and no other patient could use it, and the food was always served covered. Another unique aspect of this hospital was that patients suffering from insomnia had a place set apart for them where they were entertained with charming music and interesting stories. Very weak patients were treated to amusing plays, jokes and rural dances. The muezzins of the neighborhood were ordered to make calls for the early morning Prayer two hours ahead of the scheduled time, and recite verses with proper intonation so that the patients may be cheered and their distress may be reduced, since lack of sleep and long nights were painful for them. When the French entered Egypt in 1798, their learned men saw these things with their own eyes, and stated them in their books in detail.

It is said that in Tripoli, there was a strange trust whose income was reserved exclusively for two people who would visit the hospitals daily. Sitting beside the patients, they would speak with each other in a whisper and in such a way that the patients would overhear them, getting the impression that their health was improving; the glow of health on their faces and the brightness of their eyes appearing to be evidence of that.

It is necessary to mention here the trust deed of this magnificent hospital in its entirety, as reported by the author of *History of the Hospitals of the Islamic World*:

The opportunities of the reward of the highest acts of righteousness afforded to lofty aims, such as those which are regarded as beneficial—like the curing of such people—are acts of goodness. These acts, which have everlasting reward and bring people happiness, are based on the firm foundation of piety with aspirations of a far-reaching nature. Such acts of goodness are trusts whose beneficence is general, whose reward is abiding, whose benefits are unlimited and the reward of the Hereafter is very valuable. So these acts of goodness are the real heaven, and this is the one sacrifice that takes one to the good will and pleasure of Allah. This is the ṣadaqa which is the dower of the houris in Heaven. Consider the elation a helpless patient feels, how much support is afforded to a broken heart and how through treatment of his malady and offering him refuge he comes to feel independent. Its reward is so great that it cannot be expressed in words. Fortunate, indeed, is that person who has had such a compact with His Lord, Allah the All-Forgiving and Most Merciful. In his income and expenditure he had such a compact with Allah, who knows both one's open and hidden acts. He offered a goodly loan to Allah according to his capacity, and he valued the opportunity of surpassing others in the field of virtue. He helped a sick Muslim brother in his treatment, took away his grief; and as a reward, tomorrow, in the Court of Divine Justice, he will have deliverance from the chastisement of Hell. More than this, there is also hope of being the recipient of further exaltation in his rank and position with Allah. He will be endowed with the good fortune of closeness to Allah, where he will have no fear of any oppression or tyranny. This is such a virtuous act that will become a means of forgiveness to all his sins, and he will be free from all forms of grief. So under the urge of the attainment of these high ranks, Mālik ʿĀdil Manṣūr ordered the endowment of the Manṣūrī Hospital [here the deed of this trust mentions the endowment, their situation and particulars]. This hospital is dedicated to the treatment of the rich, the poor, men and women alike, irrespective of their place of residence, color or race. We treat whatever malady or trouble they are tormented with, whether they are physical, spiritual or nervous ailments. Those maladies may be mild or sufficiently aggravated, similar or dissimilar, apparent or concealed. They may be victims of mental aberration whose remedy is one of the most important objectives, and whose treatment is most imperative and of great importance, and can neither be overlooked nor slighted and discarded. They may also be suffering from other disorders whose early diagnosis is necessary for man. Here treatment will be undertaken with roots and herbs that are well known to the physicians. Common people, individual and collective, old and young, boys and girls will all be eligible for treatment. Indigent patients, male or female, shall stay at the hospital as inpatients for the duration of their treatment. There, they shall receive all the facilities of treatment available at the hospital and the necessities shall be distributed among all those in need of it, irrespective of them being strangers or relatives, locals or strangers on a journey here. This they shall receive, irrespective of whether they are strong or weak, from the masses or the classes, high or low, rich or poor, officer or subordinate, blind or seeing, superior or inferior, renowned or unknown, glorious or insignificant and unimportant, entrepreneur or poverty-stricken, master or slave. This treatment shall be free of charge, and nobody shall have any objection to it. This treatment shall be undertaken for the pleasure of Allah alone, attainment of the reward of the Hereafter and His Beneficence, since Allah has ordained spending for the welfare of the patient and for those who take care of the patients, such as physicians, ophthalmologists, surgeons, pharmacists, those cooking tasty and appetizing foods, those preparing electuaries, collyria men, those preparing simple and compound purgatives, postmen, treasurers, guardians or trustees, superintendents, and all workers who are employed in hospitals for various jobs; also spending on those things that are necessary for the treatment of the patient; spending on things needed for the food and the dress of the patients, lenses needed for the eyes, cauldrons and the like. Allah has also ordained spending on electuaries, various kinds of ointments, oils, drinks, simple and compound drugs, carpets and beddings, vessels and any new implementation required in this work. The manager shall have the authority to spend on the daily needs of the patients, for example, the daily expenses of incense burnt by them, the plates for food, glass tumblers to drink water and other drinks from, earthenware tumblers and goblets, earthen lamps and oil to burn in them. He shall also have the authority to spend on new implementations to procure water for drinking and cooking food from the River Nile and to purchase covers for the food offered to the patients; during summer season the date-palm leaf fans must be purchased. The superintendent or manager of the trusts shall spend on all these things from the income of the trust, but this expenditure shall not be extravagant, nor ought it waste anything wilfully, as there ought to be no excess over what is sufficient. All the expenses must be within the limits of genuine needs, so that as much as possible reward may be gained. The controller of the trusts shall appoint two persons paid from the income of this trust who must be trustworthy and honest Muslims. One of them shall hold charge of the distribution of various commodities and articles, liquid medicines, collyria, roots and herbs, electuaries, oils and wicks, and issue only those things sanctioned by the officer concerned. The other person shall distribute their particular cups to the patients, male or female, every morning and evening and give them the medicine prescribed for them. It will also be his duty to supervise the working of the kitchen where nourishing food for the patients, poultry meat, chicken and other kinds of meat, shall be prepared. It will be his duty to give every patient the food prescribed for him on a platter exclusively set apart for his use only. No other patient shall partake of that food with him. It will also be his duty to distribute properly covered food among the patients, and he shall supervise this distribution until every patient has received his prescribed food. He will be responsible for such distribution in a proper manner every morning and evening. The controller shall also have authority to appoint physicians, ophthalmologists and surgeons on reasonably lucrative remunerations. He shall determine these salaries in compliance with the existing conditions and the needs of the patients. He is fully authorized in the matter of the fixation of pay and the number of employees, but he should not allow either excess or deficiency. An attitude of moderation should be his policy. The staff shall be duty-bound to look after the conveniences and comforts of the patients all the time. As regards duty hours, they are free to either be there all at a time or take turns at it. Working hours may be fixed through mutual consultation and with the approval of the controller of endowments. It is their duty to talk to every patient and find out whether a certain patient is improving or his malady is aggravated. It should be noted properly, and with the permission of the controller of the trusts the medicines and diet of every patient should be prescribed and noted on his sheet and he should be given both according to that plan. The staff should stay at the hospital during the night, all of them together or by turns. The ophthalmologists should sit in the outpatient clinic daily and treat the patients that come to them. Every patient that comes in the morning any day of the week for getting his eyes tested and treated should under no circumstances be compelled to return disappointed. They must treat him kindly and give him the necessary aid. Those with damaged eyes and poor vision should be dealt with more courteously. If the eyes have developed wounds, the ophthalmologist should consult the surgeon in his case, taking him personally to the surgeon and not leave him to fend for himself. Even after that, the physician should keep an eye on such cases until recovery. The controller of the trusts should appoint a scholar of medicine with the income of the trust, who will, all the time, remain engaged in research, particularly in relation to the pressing problems. This expert or research officer should sit in the large consultation room that has been set apart for him in the trust deed. It will be the duty of this expert to conduct research in various branches of the medical science and the problems cropping up from day to day. The working hours for him shall be fixed by the controller of the trust according to his discretion. However, it must be kept in mind carefully that the staff should be within the limits prescribed by the trust deed. The controller of the trusts should pay reasonably good emoluments to the appointed staff of this hospital and attendants, men and women. The salaries should be in keeping with the nature of their work. This remuneration is to be paid to the attendants for their services rendered to the men and women that have been admitted to the hospital for treatment. They should also keep their place neat and tidy, wash their clothes and never mistreat the facilities and comforts provided by the hospital. These facilities too must be in keeping with the circumstances at any particular period. It is the duty of the controller of the trust that he should arrange the burial of the patients, men and women, who pass away in the hospital. They should be bathed and embalmed with aroma at the cost of the hospital. The wages of digging a grave should be met by the trust and the deceased person buried with due honors in accordance with the Sunnah of the Prophet ﷺ. The controller of the trust should supply a person, sick at home but helpless, at his residence with whichever medicine, syrup or electuary he needs. However, this should be in such a manner that the inpatients at the hospital may not suffer from a shortage of drugs. If such an outpatient dies at his own place, the keeper of the hospital should pay for his shroud, bath, digging of the grave and taking the dead body to the graveyard according to the status of the deceased. Those who are staying at the hospital and are cured by the grace of Allah, at the time of discharge they should be provided an average type of change of clothes in keeping with his status. Under this head the controller of the trust, in office, at any given time, should not go to such limits that the internal needs of the hospital may suffer for want of funds. It is, however, left to his discretion. The controller of this trust should fear Allah and consider himself responsible to men also in the discharge of his duties and never give priority to an influential person in comparison with the common people and treat him more lavishly on the basis of discrimination between the rich and poor. He should not give preference to a local patient over a foreign national, but must keep in view, in the matter of expenditure on them, the reward of the Hereafter and closeness to Allah who is the Lord of all cherishers.

4. The Moroccan Hospital

Sultan Manṣūr Abū Yūsuf, a well-known ruler of the Muwaḥiddīn Dynasty of Morocco, built this facility. Spacious land was selected in one of the most temperate places of the country and the architects and builders were ordered to make it the most beautifully designed building possible. All sorts of fruit trees and plants were grown on the premises. Canals of running water passed by every room of the hospital. Four special reservoirs were built, one of them of pure white marble. Fine beddings were provided for the hospital beds, made out of wool, linen, silk and leather. A pharmacy was built in the hospital in which different kinds of syrups, oils, collyria and other medicines were prepared. Patients were provided with different clothes for the day and night and summer and winter. Once completely cured, the poor patient would be given sufficient funds to help him start a business and earn a livelihood. A patient who was rich also received his share. This hospital was not dedicated to the poor and the indigent only, for the affluent also benefited from its existence. In whichever section of Morocco a stranger was found ill, he was brought to the hospital and admitted as an inpatient. He was either cured and discharged or died there. The Sultan would go to the hospital every Friday and learn firsthand about the health of the patients, the work of the physicians and their dealings with the patients.

These are four examples out of hundreds of hospitals that were functioning at that time in the Islamic world from the East to the West. They existed at a time when Europe was wandering under layers of darkness and was unaware of these hospitals and of their level of cleanliness and human concern. A well-known German Orientalist Dr. Marx Mayerhoff says about the European hospitals of the time, in light of the conditions in those of the Islamic Civilization, "The Arab hospitals and the health systems existing in the Islamic countries of the past is giving us a harsh and bitter lesson. We cannot fully appreciate it unless we compare this system with that of the European hospitals of that period."

About three-hundred years before our time, Europe was ignorant of the meaning of *hospital*. It would be no exaggeration to say that up to 1710 CE they were living under poor conditions. The patients were treated either at their own home or at the poorhouses in which they were kept as destitutes without any support and shelter, whether they were ill or in sound health. The best example of a European hospital was the Hospital of Otel Diew in Paris—the biggest in Europe at that time. Maxi Tordo and Tanon have both described this hospital:

> There are 1200 beds in this hospital. Out of these, 486 beds are single, one for each patient. The remainder, no more than five paces in width, were allocated between three to six patients. The extensive wards were damp, putrid and dark, with no windows or ventilators, and had more than 800 patients lying on the ground. There was hardly room for them to lie down comfortably, so they were miserably huddled up on the bare ground or on a heap of rubbish! A pitiable sight indeed for any person with human feelings. On an average bed, five or six patients were lying in a heap, the feet of one over the head of another, the young in the company of the old, women by the side of men. Although it violates common sense, it is the truth. On the one side there is a woman menstruating and by her side was a child suffering from typhoid and in a state of convulsion and burning with fever. Both of these are in turn lying with a victim of a skin infection scratching his dying skin with his equally dirty blood stained nails, and pus is spilled on the bed which cannot be soiled any further. The quality of food given to them were as bad as could be conceived, and that too in a very meagre quantity and irregularly after long intervals. The nuns supervising the working of the hospital had a preference for the rich patients who were provided with wine at the expense of the poor patients. Sometimes they gave the sweet dishes and other rich

> foods, received as alms, to such patients for whom they were detrimental due to their peculiar maladies. Some of them died of overeating, indigestions, even cholera, while others died of starvation. The doors of this hospital were always open. In this way diseases could spread outside the hospital. There was human excretion and the air was heavy laden with noxious odours. Food arrangements were limited wholly to alms. If the rich people had not sent cooked food to the hospital, the inmates would have died of starvation, as some of them died of overeating and drinking heavily. The bedding was teeming with insects and even vermin. The atmosphere of these wards was so foul that the nurses and attendants found it difficult to enter even after putting pieces of cloth moistened with vinegar to their noses. If a patient died there, his corpse would not be removed from the hospital bed for at least twenty-four hours. At times such corpses got bloated and began to rot and stink, but still lay by the side of another patient on the same bed who would find himself nearer death due to this agonizingly foul atmosphere.

This shows what abysmal depths of degradation due to ignorance and utter lack of knowledge of the principles, rules and regulations for the management of hospitals the European nations had once lived in. They had no prior knowledge of the existence of any such principles of public health and hygiene. Rather, they were ignorant of even the most apparent principles of the aspects of health that common sense suggests, for which no education and training were necessary. The famous physician Usāma ibn Munqaz, narrates two events in his book *al-Iʿtibār* which gives an idea of the knowledge of medical science of the Christians of the West. He says:

> Among the marvels of the medical affairs is that Sāḥib Munitrah wrote to his uncle saying that there was need of a doctor to treat his companions. My uncle sent a Christian doctor, Thābit, to them, but he came back within ten days. We asked him, "Were you able to treat the patients in such a short period?" He said, "They had brought to me a soldier who had a boil on one of his feet. When a bandage dipped in the juice of a plant was applied, the abscess burst. There was another patient, a woman whose dry and chapped skin had developed an itch and was giving her trouble. I kept her on a restricted diet as a preventive measure and tried to make her dry skin moist. But suddenly an English doctor appeared on the scene and told the people there about me, 'What does he know of medical science and treatment of patients?' He then asked the soldier with the abscess on his foot whether he would like to live with one leg or die with both. The soldier said he would prefer to live with one leg only. So the soldier and a sharp axe were brought and I was a witness to the scene. The English doctor straightened his leg on a wooden board and asked the soldier to chop off his leg with a single stroke of his axe. He made a stroke with the axe, and found that it failed to sever the leg. So he made a second attempt. The bone marrow was thrown out and the patient died immediately.

The author then relates in great detail how the English doctor poured boiling water on the woman and she too died immediately.

In conclusion, we can say that the Islamic Civilization established the highest standard in the field of the management of hospitals about nine hundred years prior to Western Civilization. The hospitals of the Islamic Civilization were established under such exalted human sentiments and principles of mercy and justice to humanity, which have no parallel in history. Furthermore, these sentiments and principles have not yet been fully witnessed to this day in the Western countries.

Muslims were the first nation to discover the effects on the patient's psychological consciousness of melody and humorous literature through experimentation. This proved to be very helpful in the treatment of diseases. Muslims have established such a high record in the matter of collective support not attained even in this advanced age. The patients were treated free of charge and their board and lodge were also arranged free. After being cured, the poor and the destitute were also given enough money to help them earn their livelihood during the rest of their lives.

This high position of philanthropy was attained when the banner of leadership was in the hands of Muslims in the then civilized world. However, where are the Muslims today?

CHAPTER ELEVEN

PRIVATE AND PUBLIC LIBRARIES

THERE WERE NUMEROUS schools for education and training. Leaders, the affluent and the scholars used to spend their money on such institutions for the spread of knowledge among the people, especially in that period when printing and publishing facilities were not available and books used to be copied at the hands of the scribes—specialists in that field. Thus, the price of a book would be too expensive for a student of knowledge or a poor scholar to buy. There was no question of acquiring a collection of books in a particular field of knowledge one was concerned with. This is why libraries were established in Muslim societies—a result of purely human sentiments and at the same time academic inclination and interests.

Perhaps Arabic literature is the richest of the ancient literatures. Here, everyone appears to be a lover of books; books are being discussed and every one is interested in books. It appears as if the book was a lover whom one had not met for a long time. Aḥmad ibn Ismāʿīl says, "The book is a companion in conversation, and does not trouble you by broaching topics while you are busy, and does not put you to inconvenience by calling on you at the time of your respite [from work] or rest. When you want to see and talk to him you need no elaborate preparations to do so. The book is a friend that does not praise you to the skies, does not deceive you, and a companion that does not grieve you; it is an advisor that protects you from stumbling into error."

Muslim men of letters preferred the study of books to gatherings and discussions, for being close to books was closer to their hearts than being close to the Caliph or the Ruler. When al-Jāḥiẓ wanted to visit Muḥammad ibn ʿAbd al-Mālik al-Ziyāt, a literary figure and a minister, he thought the best gift to give him would be the book by Sībawayh, the master Arabist of his time. The minister accepted the gift joyfully and said to al-Jāḥiẓ, "By Allah! Nobody ever gave me a gift more beloved than this gift of yours."

One of the Caliphs sent for a certain scholar to speak to him. When the servant found the scholar, he found him sitting and engrossed in reading, with many books around him. He said to him, "You have been called by the Amīr al-Mu'minīn." He replied, "Tell him that I am presently in the company of great learned men and philosophers and engaged in conversation with them. When I have finished with them, I will come and see him." The servant returned and informed the Caliph. He asked the servant, "Who are those learned men and philosophers engaged in conversation with him?" The servant replied, "By Allah, O Amīr al-Mu'minīn! I did not see anyone there." The Caliph said, "Bring him here at once." When he came, the Caliph asked him, "Who were those learned men who were keeping you company." He replied, "O Amīr al-Mu'minīn.

They are companions whose talk does not bore you. Present or absent they are constant and trustworthy. When we are in seclusion their talk is very beneficial and helpful in taking away anxieties and worries. They benefit us with their knowledge—knowledge of what has passed—with wisdom, affability, prudence and sound opinion. You will neither have any apprehension nor fear of discourtesy, nor dread of any injury from their hand or their tongue. If I said that they are dead, I would not be a liar. And if I say they are living, I would not be lying." The Caliph did not reprimand him for not responding to his call immediately.

Ṣāḥib ibn ʿUbād, instead of accepting the highest post in the royal palace of Nūḥ ibn Manṣūr al-Samanī, opted for the company of books in a library, since he was in love with his library, he could not leave it and could not take it with him. So he preferred to live where his heart was. This was the spirit of the learning on whose basis our learned men, the rich and the noble, showed such zealous attachment to books and collected them. They considered the loss of their domestic goods much less than the loss of books.

Once during a war, Ibn al-Amid's house was attacked by an army and his slaves and guards were taken prisoners. Ibn al-Amid himself fled to Dār al-Imāra. The army plundered his house completely. On returning home, he found every thing was gone, and there was neither anything to sit on nor a cup to drink water from. But in spite of all this, he had no cause for worry save the anxiety for his books, the most cherished part of his belongings. He had in his library books of which he had no count, all subjects of various disciplines including literature and philosophy. They could hardly be loaded on a hundred camels. When Ibn al-Amid saw his librarian, he asked him about his books. He told him that the library was untouched. Ibn al-Amid's face brightened with a glow of happiness and said to the librarian, "I bear witness to the fact that you are a dutiful guard. All other kinds of goods can be replaced but not this stock of books."

With this spirit of learning, people would compete with each other in purchasing books. As soon as a book neared completion, people approached the author or compiler to buy it. For example, the ruler of Andalusia, Ḥakam, learnt that Abū al-Faraj Aṣfahānī was writing his famous literary book *al-Aghānī*. He sent him a thousand dinars as the price of one copy of this book and asked him to send it as soon as it was completed. So this book found its way to Andalusia and was being read there long before being available in his own country—Iraq.

Due to this literary taste and spirit of learning, libraries were established throughout different parts of the Islamic world. There were few schools that did not have libraries of their own, and there were few towns or villages without libraries. As for the larger towns and the capital, the libraries were in such abundance that there was nothing similar even in the Middle Ages.

The libraries were primarily of two kinds—public and private. Public libraries were established by the Caliphs, nobles, scholars and the rich. Separate permanent buildings were built for them, and at times, these libraries were annexed to the large mosques or schools.

As for the independent and permanent library buildings, they comprised several rooms and spacious halls which connected these rooms. The books were kept on shelves fixed along the walls. Every room was set apart for books on a particular discipline. For example, there was a room for books of jurisprudence, a room for books on medicine, and a room for books on literature and so on.

In this building there were separate rooms for those wanting to read in the library [that is, reading rooms] and there were rooms for the scribes who used to copy books. In some library buildings, there was a separate room for music where the students could go to relax and refresh themselves—this is an aspect unique to Islamic Civilization. There were also rooms in which the learned men would gather for academic discussions and studies. All these rooms were furnished with the best and most comfortable furniture. There were separate rooms that served as dining halls for those coming to the library so that they could stay there for prolonged study. For the visitors, there were bedrooms where they could sleep, as reported in connection with the library of ᶜAlī ibn Yaḥyā ibn al-Munajjim who had a magnificent castle in the vicinity of Qafs, close to Baghdad in the village of Karkar. In the castle, he had a large great library known as "Treasures of Wisdom," where people would come from near and far and where they would stay to study the various disciplines. They would be provided with books and all the expenses were paid for by ᶜAlī ibn Yaḥyā himself.

There were some facilities available at these libraries which do not compare with the capitals of the most advanced countries of Western Civilization. Abū al-Qāsim Jaᶜfar ibn Muḥammad

Ḥamdān al-Mūṣūlī had built a house in Mūṣūl that he had named "House of Knowledge." He dedicated it a large library, with books in every discipline. No one was prevented from entering and, if a poor student came to it with the goal of acquiring knowledge, he was supplied not only with stationery for his work, but also a fairly decent stipend for his expenses. This library was open everyday of the week.

In the public libraries a full-time staff was employed. The head librarian was known as the *Khāzin al-Maktabah.* He would always be a renowned scholar of the time. There were also people who delivered the books to the readers. The translators would be transferring books from other languages into Arabic whilst the scribes would be writing books with their beautiful calligraphy. The binders would be binding books to save them from getting damaged or lost. Over and above these well-known posts, there were people employed for other miscellaneous jobs of a minor nature.

Every big and small library had a catalogue of books with which any book could be taken out easily. This catalogue was prepared according to the disciplines to which the books belonged. Every bookcase would have its own list with all the books present in it. In most libraries the general people could borrow books by depositing the requisite security for them. However, the scholars and others known for their excellence in learning and honor were exempt from this rule and no deposit was demanded of them.

The sources of the income of these libraries varied. For most of the public libraries, there were trusts built exclusively for their maintenance. The nobles, the rich and the scholars financed other libraries. It is said that Muḥammad ibn ʿAbd al-Mālik al-Ziyāt used to pay two thousand dinars monthly to the copyists and the calligraphists. Ma'mūn al-Rashīd paid Ḥunayn ibn Isḥāq the weight in gold of every book Ḥunayn rendered into Arabic from other languages.

It would be appropriate to mention here some of the public and private libraries that have been mentioned in history:

1. Maktabat al Khulafā' al-Fāṭmiyyah, Cairo

This library of the Fatimid Caliphs of Cairo was one of the most famous one of that time. This was a wonderful library containing the finest copies of the Quran and other books, of which there were 2 million in number, although Maqrizī is of the opinion that it comprised 1.6 million books.

2. Dār al-Ḥikma, Cairo

Instituted by Ḥakīm ibn Amrullāh, this library was inaugurated on 10th Jumāda of 365 AH, when its building was decorated and the floor draped with the best carpets, and the supervisory and managerial staff assigned. It was a magnificent collection of books, quite unlike any that a monarch had made before. It had forty sections, each comprising eighteen thousand books, including all kinds on ancient sciences and arts. It was open to everyone. Some people would go there for study, others to copy books and yet others only to acquire knowledge. Stationery of every description was supplied to the visitors of this library free of charge.

3. Bayt al Ḥikma, Baghdad

Another such library was Bayt al Ḥikma of Baghdad, founded by Hārūn al-Rashīd which reached its peak during the rule of Ma'mūn al-Rashīd. It was similar to a university where people would discuss, read and write together. It used to have scribes and translators who would translate books acquired by Hārūn al-Rashīd and Ma'mūn al-Rashīd after the Conquests of Ankara, Amūriyyah and Cyprus. Ibn Nadīm related that there was lengthy correspondence between Ma'mūn al-Rashīd and the Roman King whom he had defeated in some battles. One of the conditions of the treaty between them was that the Roman King would allow the translation of all the books in his dominion and the translation work would be undertaken by those whom Ma'mūn would appoint for this purpose. So it was, and the entire Roman stock of books was rendered into Arabic. It is a golden example in history that a conqueror gave no greater importance to a conquest than the transfer of sciences and arts for the benefit of his people and his nation.

4. Maktabah al-Ḥakam, Andalusia

This library was very spacious and magnificent. It is said to have comprised 250,000 books. Its catalogues were very nicely prepared and gave every detail so much so that the catalogue of the collections of the poetical works alone comprised forty-four sections. The expert scribes were permanently employed there. Similarly, the services of the book binders were also available, with the result that Andalusia came to have a larger stock of books than ever before or ever since.

5. Maktabah Banī ʿAmmār, Tripoli

This library was a sign from the signs of Allah in terms of its spaciousness and grandiosity. The number of scribes alone was one hundred and eighty, who copied books within the stipulated time. They had shifts of duties around the clock, so that the copying business might continue uninterrupted. Banū ʿAmmār had such avidity for collecting new and rare books that he employed some officers and traders to tour different parts of their own country and also other countries to collect books for their library. Opinions differ regarding the number of books in this library although an accurate opinion is that it comprised a million books.

The Islamic world was full of private libraries, both in the East and West. There was hardly any learned man not possessing a library of his own comprising thousands of books:

1. Library of Fattāḥ ibn Khaqān

Among such personal libraries that of Fattāḥ ibn Khaqān (d. 247 AH) is very well known. It was a very spacious library. He had appointed the best learned man of his age, ʿAlī ibn Yaḥyā al-Munajjim, to look for and collect books. These books were not to be found elsewhere.

2. Library of Ibn Khashshāb

The library of Ibn Khashshāb (d. 567 CE) also comes under this category of libraries. He was an expert in *naḥw* [syntax] and had good knowledge of *tafsīr* [Quranic commentary], hadith, logic and also philosophy. His love of books touched the limits of madness. This mad love for books compelled him to take to certain evil practices also in the collection of books. When he went to the bookseller and wanted to purchase any good book he would tear off certain pages of that book by stealth while pretending to examine it and then compelled the bookseller to sell the damaged book at a much cheaper price. Similarly, when he borrowed a book from some friend, he would usually pretend to have misplaced it and then keep it for himself.

3. Library of Jamāluddīn al-Qiftī

The library of Jamāluddīn al-Qiftī (d. 648 AH) was famous. He collected innumerable books. Due to his generosity, people from all sides would come to his place. Books were his first and last love, almost his craze, and he had dedicated his life to them. For this reason he did not marry because of the apprehension of being entangled in managing a house and looking after a family. At the time of his death he bequeathed his collection of books to Nāṣir. It was worth fifty-thousand dinars.

4. Library of Banū Jaradah.

The library of the learned men of Banū Jaradah of Aleppo is also famous. One of these persons, Abū al-Ḥasan ibn Abī Jaradah (d. 548 AH) wrote books to fill three libraries with his own hand—one for himself, one for his son Abū Barakāt and a third for his grandson ʿAbdullāh.

5. Library of Mawfīq ibn al-Matrān

Mawfīq ibn al-Matrān Damishqī (d. 587 CE) also had a famous library. He showed great fortitude and ambition in the procurement of books. At his death his collection of books on medical sciences and other disciplines comprised ten-thousand volumes. He had employed three scribes who were always busy copying books for his library. He paid them salaries and provided other necessities also.

If the hearts are filled with happiness when discussing the spread of libraries across the Islamic world in the glory days, then it should be filled with sadness and remorse when discussing the fate of these libraries as they were exposed to ruin and fire, the loss of which cannot be counted. Millions of books were destroyed and humanity is now deprived of them. It was the most expensive intellectual tradition of Islamic Civilization.

The calamity of the Tartars when they entered Baghdad afflicted those libraries before anything else. It is well known that the barbarian Tartars would throw books that they came across into the River Tigris until the river waters became so shallow that they were crossed easily by their horsemen, not in a single file but in whole ranks. For months, the water of the river had a black tinge due to the ink washed off the pages of the books.

Later, calamities visited the Islamic world through the Crusades which destroyed all the precious libraries of Tripoli, Ma'arrah, Bayt al-Maqdis, ʿAsqalān and other big cities, since after the conquest, the cities themselves had been razed to the ground. The historians have recorded that in Tripoli alone the

Crusaders destroyed three million books. This is a clear indication of the magnitude of this destruction.

The domination of Andalusia by the Spaniards deprived humanity of so many magnificent libraries. An idea of the damage done by these fanatical religious people in making fires of books can be gauged by the fact that in one open space of Granada alone, one million books were burnt in a single day.

These are some of the mass destruction of the great libraries of the Islamic world wrought by the enemies of Islam. However, the internal conflicts of the Islamic Civilization did no less damage. The library of the Fatimid Caliph of Egypt ended at the hands of the Turkish Slave Dynasty when they came to dominate Egypt. They destroyed it completely by setting fire to it. They tore away the fine leather in which the books were bound and made shoes out of it. Innumerable books were thrown into the Nile. Some books were taken away by people to various distant parts of the country, while the remaining were heaped in the open fields to rot and their pages were torn one by one by the winds.

Aleppo had a great library known as *Khazānat al-Ṣūfiyyah.* On the occasion of ʿAshūrā', a Shīʿa-Sunnī riot broke out and people destroyed it almost completely. The library of Mustanṣir, the ruler of Andalusia, met its destruction at the hands of Berber tribes when they entered as conquerors. They sold many books and the remaining ones were destroyed.

The most amazing calamity of all, ludicrous as it may be, is what a stupid person does with knowledge. Amīr ibn Fatik, a leader of Egypt in the fifth century after *hijrah*, had a huge library.

He used to sit in there most of his time and would not leave it. He had a wife who belonged to a very respectable family but who abhorred these books. When Ibn Fatik passed away, she and her neighbors entered the library and started throwing the books into a tank of water in their open courtyard. She was also lamenting her husband's loss but said during the wailing that these books held his attention most of the time and did not let him attend to her. This was the revenge wreaked on the books that were the first love of her husband. The wife of Imām al-Zuhrī on finding her husband engrossed in books, used to say, By Allah! These books are heavier on me than three rival women.

This is the woeful tale of the demise of the libraries in the Islamic world during the period of Islamic Civilization. Although it is difficult to forgive what the enemy has done, it is the duty of Muslims to do so with an open heart and know that the role of books in Europe has preserved a fairly large number of the legacies of Islamic Civilization. These libraries contain, to this day, those treasures of the Arabic literature, the likes of which are not to be found anywhere in the entire Islamic world.

CHAPTER TWELVE

SOCIETIES AND ACADEMIC CIRCLES

SOCIETIES AND ACADEMIC circles are a bright aspect of the magnificent Islamic Civilization which have had a beneficial effect in spreading culture, knowledge and learning. It raised the cultural level and developed the academic taste of the people. The societies and academic circles were common in the Muslim capitals and other big cities along with an abundance of schools, academic institutions and libraries. The multitude and variety of their discussions were a great manifestation of the intellectual awakening during the glory and splendour of the Muslim *Ummah*. There was a diverse range of classes among the Caliphs, nobles, leaders, scholars, men of letters and poets holding academic, literary and philosophical competitions in their private and public gatherings. This shows that the Muslim *Ummah* had reached a level of passion for knowledge and thirst that could not be satisfied and it also proves the greatness and progress of Islamic Civilization.

These societies were numerous and various and some were under the control of the Caliphs who presided over them. They were attended by the most renowned scholars, men of letters and jurists. The circles developed with the progress and cultural growth of Islamic Civilization. At the time of the Rightly Guided Caliphs, discussions on the State, governance and many other issues used to take place in these circles. ᶜUmar ibn al-Khaṭṭāb once needed someone to supervise some important work of the State, thus he said to those in the circle, "Tell me who I can use for an important task." They suggested someone, but he said, "We don't need him." They asked, "Who do you want then?" He said, "I want a man who, if he is with a group of people of whom he is not their leader, he acts as though he is their leader; and if he is their leader then he acts as though he is one of them." They said, "We don't know of anyone fitting this description except Rabīᶜ ibn Ziyād al-Ḥārithī." He said, "You have spoken truthfully." Thus Rabīᶜ was appointed.

During the period of the Umayyads, these societies became circles of literature, logic, wisdom and poetry. Once ᶜAbdullāh ibn Hāshim came to a gathering chaired by Muᶜāwiyyah and the latter asked, "Who can define generosity, courage and valour for me?" ᶜAbdullāh replied, "O Amīr al-Mu'minīn! Generosity is giving charity before it is requested. Courage is going forth and standing one's ground firmly when a slip appears imminent. Valour is righteousness in the religion and reforming one's self, and supporting the neighbor."

ᶜAbd al-Mālik asked the audience in a gathering, "Who among you can present such words relating to the human body, which begin with letters in the alphabetical order? I shall give that person whatever he wants as a reward." Suwayd ibn Ghaflah said to him, "I will, O Amīr al-Mu'minīn." ᶜAbd al-Mālik granted him permission and he said, "*Anf* [nose], *Baṭn* [abdomen], *Tarqutah* [clavicle], *Thaghr* [front teeth or incisors], *Jamjamah* [skull], *Ḥalq* [throat], *Khad*, [cheek]" and so on. Another man volunteered to present a double set of such words. On this Suwayd said he could treble the list. So he said, "*Anf* [nose], *Asnān* [teeth], *Udhun* [ears] and continued giving three words each for the next letters of the alphabet. ʿAbd al-Mālik was amazed at his spontaneous intuition and thus rewarded him.

A Bedouin once came to ʿAbd al-Mālik while he was sitting in a gathering in which the poet Jarīr was present. ʿAbd al-Mālik said to the Bedouin, "Do you know anything about poetry?" He said, "Ask me whatever you like, O Amīr al-Mu'minīn." ʿAbd al-Mālik asked him, "Which is the best verse in the field of praise?" The Bedouin said, "The saying of Jarīr: 'Are you not the best amongst those who have ridden a mount? / And are you not more generous than the whole world?'" Jarīr raised his head and kept it raised. Then ʿAbd al-Mālik asked the Bedouin, "Which is the best couplet in the field of honor and pride?" The Bedouin said, "The saying of Jarīr: 'When the people of Banū Tamīm are angry with you, / You will think that everyone is angry with you.'"

Jarīr was ecstatic, moving his head from side to side. ʿAbd al-Mālik said, "Which is the best couplet in the field of satire?" The Bedouin replied, "The saying of Jarīr: 'Lower your gaze for you are from Banī Numayr. / You will never be able to raise to the position of Kaʿb or Kilāb [famous tribes].'"

Jarīr's face glowed. ʿAbd al-Mālik then asked him, 'Which couplet is the best in the field of love?' The Bedouin said, "The saying of Jarīr: 'The eyes, whose beauty slew us, / Yet did not resurrect us.'"

Jarīr was now ecstatic beyond measure. ʿAbd al-Mālik said, "Which is the couplet in which the best simile has been used?" The Bedouin said, "The saying of Jarīr: "Night approached towards them, whose stars appeared / To be entwined wicks burning in chandeliers.'"

Jarīr, who was now very proud and delighted, said, "O Amīr al-Mu'minīn! Confer my pay to this Bedouin." ʿAbd al-Mālik said in reply, "He too will receive just as much, without any deduction in yours." The Bedouin left with 8,000 dirhams in his right hand and a package of clothes in his left hand.

During the ʿAbbāsid period, these sittings and gatherings improved. It was the best of gatherings in terms of its furniture, spaciousness, multitude of scholars, men of letters and variety of discussion. These were over and above those sittings organized for mere pleasure which were characterized by a literary color, and in which poetry, poets and explanations of words that the singers sing came up for discussion.

Among the ʿAbbāsid Caliphs, Rashīd and Ma'mūn were renowned for their very extensive and magnificent gatherings. Hārūn al-Rashīd had gathered around himself many great scholars in every branch of learning and arts. The outstanding poets of his court were Abū Nawās, Abū al-Itahiyyah, Da'bal, Muslim ibn al-Walīd and ʿAbbās ibn al-Asnaf. Among the jurists were Abū Yūsuf, al-Shāfiʿī, Muḥammad ibn al-Ḥasan. Among the grammarians and linguists were Abū ʿUbayda, al-Asmāʿī and al-Kasā'ī and among the historians, the world famous al-Wāqidī.

Among the commentators of the Quran there were Ibrāhīm al-Mūṣalī and his son Isḥāq.

There are many examples of the literary discussions. In one of the literary sittings Kasā'ī and Sībawayh and other leading scholars in the field of language and literature had gathered. Kasā'ī was of the opinion that the Arabs used an idiom like this: "I used to think that sting of the hornet was more painful than that of bee / so now it has become certain that it is so." [The idiom and the debate surrounding it can be understood only in the original Arabic.]

Sībawayh differed with Kasā'ī on the correct idiom. Long and tiring discussions on this continued between them but without any outcome. Finally it was agreed upon that a pure Bedouin Arab, whose language had not been corrupted by the language of the city dwellers, would be called to pronounce judgement. Hārūn al-Rashīd had great regard for Kasā'ī, for he had been his teacher before Hārūn became Caliph. Hārūn had a Bedouin called from the desert, who pronounced it the way Sībawayh pronounced it. Hārūn said to him, "We need you to pronounce it the way Kasā'ī pronounced it." The Bedouin replied, "My tongue does not comply with that." Finally he agreed to judge between Kasā'ī and Sībawayh when they both pronounced it before him and would decide in favor of Kasā'ī. Thus this took place in a full gathering and Sībawayh learned that they were favoring Kasā'ī. He became dejected and left Baghdad. It is said that he did not live long after this incident and that grief caused his death.

Similarly, issues of jurisprudence were also discussed in the circles of Hārūn. One of the most interesting of such polemical contests was that a disciple of Imām Abū Ḥanīfah, Imām Muḥammad ibn al-Ḥasan, said that Kasā'ī was not an expert of *Fiqh* [jurisprudence] as he had limited knowledge of the Arabic language. Kasā'ī said that a person attaining perfection in any one discipline can see his way through others with insight. Imām Muḥammad tested him by asking him, "If a person falls into error while rectifying an error in Prayer, is he required to repeat twice the rectifying prostration?" Kasā'ī said, "No." Imām Muḥammad asked, "Why?" He replied, "The grammarians say that once a word had been in a diminutive form, it cannot further be submitted to this operation a second time."

In the history of the academic circles of Islamic Civilization, the sittings of the scholars around Ma'mūn al-Rashīd were magnificent, since he was a high-ranking scholar in his own right. There was always a large gathering of scholars, men of letters, poets, physicians and great philosophers, in his palace. He had brought these men to the capital from various places, and he favored them without any distinction of race or creed. Many times he would start the discussion and thus prompt the scholars to participate in the discussions and debates. He would forbid the scholars and the philosophers from bringing up arguments from their religious books. He used to say to them, "Don't derive evidence from the Quran or the Bible; thinking that you would draw closer to me." What he intended to do was to avoid engendering religious polemics in these sittings of purely academic interest, and the gatherings comprised people with varying thoughts and creeds. In the well-known debate on the "creation" of the Quran between the jurists and scholars of hadith, he participated personally, which testifies to the extent of his knowledge in the various disciplines of *Sharīᶜah*. This also shows how well-versed he was in the knowledge of the Quranic verses and the traditions of the Prophet ﷺ which are the two major sources of the injunctions of the *Sharīᶜah*. There were fixed rules for the debates in these gatherings and all the participants abided by them. For example, the debater should not show signs of anger, should not be surprised, should not shout at his adversary and should not appeal to any one else for appreciation of his point. As long as he was speaking, there should be no other aim except for the search for Truth and seeking the path of rectitude.

Similarly, when we proceed from the ᶜAbbāsid Caliphs and come to the learned gatherings of the Fatimids of Cairo, we find the same grandeur. The capital had a large number of scholars gathered for discussions on topics of academic interest, and often the Caliphs themselves presided over these sittings.

In addition to those circles held at the Caliph's courts, there were private gatherings of the ministers and nobles at which scholars of all disciplines would gather. The accounts of the learned gatherings of al-Baramakah fill the pages of history and literature. Discussions and debates on topics of academic interest were held in these meetings. In the gatherings of Sayf al-Dawlah Ḥamdānī, only poets participated and numbered more than forty. The renowned poet Mutanabbī was also a participant. These gatherings reminded people of the magnificent gatherings of the ministers of the golden period of the ᶜAbbāsids. The same is said of the gatherings of the minister Ibn al-Gharat. Abū Ḥayyān Tawḥīdī has mentioned these gatherings, presided over by the minister in his book, *al-Amta wa'l-Muwānisāt*. Those participating in these meetings were Sirānī, Khālidī, Qudāmah ibn Jaᶜfar, ᶜAlī ibn ᶜĪsā al-Jarrāḥ, and many other famous philosophers and logicians. Abū Ḥayyān has also mentioned his own learned gatherings with the minister Abū ᶜAbdullāh Ḥusayn ibn Sadān Samsam al-Dawlah.

Apart from the circles of the Caliphs, the nobles and the ministers, there were also academic circles among the scholars, men of letters and common people. Suffice it is to mention one such gatherings.

Once, the well known man of letters Ibn al-Muqaffa, and the famous scholars and literati, gathered together in one sitting. Ibn al-Muqaffa, a Persian, put this question to the gathering, "Who are the wisest people in the world?" In deference to his feelings, they said that the Persians were the wisest people in the world. Ibn al-Muqaffa said, "No, never. They neither have abstruseness of thought, nor have they the erudite among them. They neither have this capability, nor can that excellence be for them. They are certainly people given to the pursuit of knowledge. Others bring in new ideas and by raising new points put fresh interpretations on known facts, but they can only choose from them and follow them. They themselves are incapable of deduction." At this, those gathered there said, "It is the Romans then." But Ibn al-Muqaffa replied, "They certainly have very sturdy bodies and are well versed in geometry and architecture, but nothing more." Then somebody said, "It must be the Chinese then." Ibn al-Muqaffa said, "They are only artisans and craftsmen. What have they got to do with such intellectual pursuits and thought?" Somebody suggested that it must be the Turks. But Ibn al-Muqaffa said, "They are only hunting animals." What he meant to suggest was that they knew nothing but fighting. Somebody said, 'It is the people of Hind then.' Ibn al-Muqaffa said, "They are extremely superstitious and are cunning and vicious conjurers." Tired of his attitude and their own helplessness, they asked him to tell them himself. And in reply he said, "It is the Arabs." The audience started whispering, since they could not expect a person of Persian extraction to give preference to Arabs over all other nations of the world. Ibn al-Muqaffa became angry over this reaction of theirs and said, "Do you take me for a flatterer? By God! I did not say it to please you. I am asserting that in spite of being a non-Arab, I should not deprive myself of recognizing an evident truth." Then he went on to give reasons for the superiority of the Arabs over all other nations of the world, in great detail, "They were living in a region where there was no revealed Book, nor were there sciences and arts present at the time. Despite this, they made certain findings in the vegetation of the earth and determined which of the growths were useful for goats and which for the camels. Due to variations of seasons, they determined which crops were summer crops and winter crops, and summer and winter seasons. The gained from rains, knowledge of seasonal changes. They used the stars for their journeys by land and sea. They formulated principles to keep away from evil and to side with the good which prompted them to lofty moral acts and guarded them against lowness. So much so, the poverty-stricken Bedouin living in distant parts of the wilderness comes to define morality and goes into the finest details of morals. Similarly, when he comes to speak against the detriment of evil, he does full justice to the topic. Remnants of their poetical works that lie before us contain teachings of lofty morals and righteousness, protection of the neighbor and generosity and development of agreeable moral traits. Each one of them arrived at these conclusions only due to their mental exercises, inquiry and intelligence and was unaided by acquired knowledge. They had never come by any precedent or education. That is why I told you that the Arabs were, by birth, given to temperateness, right thinking and sound judgment, and were quick witted."

One should not forget the role of the Muslim booksellers in the Islamic Civilization, who were called the *Warrāq*. Their places too were centres where the scholars, men of letters and other educated people gathered. Here everyone could attend meetings on their own particular interest and relating to their branch of learning. Most of the booksellers were men of letters and educated people in their own right. Their vocation served to quench their thirst for learning. Ibn Nadīm, author of *Kitāb al-Fahrist*, and Yāqūt, author of *Muᶜjam al-Udāba* and *Muᶜjam al-Buldān*, were both booksellers. Abū al-Faraj Aṣfahānī, author of *Aghānī*, and Abū Naṣr al-Zujāj frequented the booksellers and would meet each other there. They both held discussions on poetry and literature with the poets coming to these bookshops. In one such sitting, Abū al-Ḥasan ᶜAlī ibn Yūsuf, a poet, was at

Abū al-Fattāḥ ibn al-Hazzāz's shop reciting the couplets of Ibrāhīm ibn ʿAbbās Sawlī, "He saw my love in such a way that its place of hiding was concealed from view. / It remained as dust in his eyes, until it was revealed."

When Abū al-Fattāḥ recited this couplet, Abū al-Ḥasan liked it very much and had it repeated. Abū Naṣr al-Zujjāj says, "Abū al-Faraj asked me to say to Abū al-Ḥasan that he praised the couplet extravagantly. It must be admitted that it is a fine composition. However, he should point out its most excellent feature [the figure of speech used]." Abū Naṣr says that he went to Abū al-Ḥasan and put that question to him, to which he replied, "'It remained the straw of his eye' has a lot of beauty in it. He sent me to him once again to point out his error and tell him that all the beauty lay in the phrase "its place of hiding was concealed from view."

It was on account of this utility of the bookshops in the field of learning that some men of letters have said, "To sit in the markets is regarded bad manners, but there are sittings in the market that are useful. So do not even approach the gatherings of the market except those of the horses, arms and the books, for the first two will give you the means of combat and the last one will arm you with literary weapons."

The need for weapons and war and the need for knowledge and literature is the need of every noble man who wants to live a life honor, dignity and nobility.

The nation that deserves life finds its food in knowledge before everything else. When the Muslim *Ummah* was infusing life into the nations of the world, it had tread every path for increasing knowledge and spreading it. It left no stone unturned in the field of propagation of sciences and arts. Rather, all the sons of the Islamic faith, from the Caliph to the learned men and even the traders, were busy competing with each other in propagating knowledge, constructing schools and providing all the facilities in this field. In the schools, the lessons and the discussions gave the students great vision and developed their intellect. Even in their gatherings of amusement, they were scholars and men of letters and would find solutions to problems, clarify ambiguities or correct mistakes.

The circles of the jurists, scholars of tradition and preachers have not been discussed since they were so commonly held in every village and town and were well known. In short, the Islamic Civilization, in its days of glory, had illumined the Islamic world with the light of knowledge and culture. This illumination had extended to the homes, mosques, schools, private assemblies, gatherings and shops. The great scholar Gustav Labon rightly said, "The Arabs had a great love for learning. In a very brief span of time they accomplished their conquest, and then turning to civilization and culture attained a very lofty position and gave birth to a civilization whose science, arts, poetry and literature matured to reach their climax."

CHAPTER THIRTEEN

CAPITALS AND LARGE CITIES

WHEN COMPARING THE cities of Islamic Civilization and the cities of the Western world, one will find great differences between the two. One found a world full of life, vitality and civilization—the Islamic world—and in the Western world a primal realm with hardly any traces of life, knowledge or civilization. As regards the Western world and the standard of living of its inhabitants and the expansion of its cities, La Face and Rombo wrote:

> The Anglo-Saxon England of the seventh to the tenth century and even later, was a very poor country, cut off from the rest of the world. Ignorance, vulgarity and barbarism were rampant. Houses were built of unhewn stone, cemented together with mud. And the floors were also plastered with mud. The houses were small and their outlets and ventilators were narrow, the doors very fragile and the animal enclosures entirely lacking in windows or ventilators. Cattle, which were the only wealth of the land, were dying constantly due to many diseases and epidemics. The people themselves did not live any better than the animals and when it came to the dwelling and shelter, the condition of the people themselves was no happier than that of their

animals. The head of the family lived in a hut with his family, servants and others connected with him. All these people would gather together in a large hall in the middle of which there was a stove sending smoke to a hole in the roof. They would all eat from the same plate with the head of the family and his wife occupying one end of the table. Knifes and forks were unknown in those days and the bowls were pointed at the bottom and had to be held in the hands or the person eating had to take its contents at a gulp. Having had their dinner early in the evening they would quarrel over the drink. After that every one took his pillow and sword and slept on the floor or on a bench and kept his weapon handy since robbery was common and everyone had to remain alert. Europe at that time was covered with dense forests. Agriculture was in a primitive stage. Around the towns there were pools of stagnant dirty water, whose noxious odour made the atmosphere stinking all round, and people fell prey to so many diseases and died in large numbers. In Paris and London the houses were built with mud mixed with straw and wood. There were neither windows nor doors in their rooms and bedding was something unknown to them. They had no bedding except straw upon which they would lay on the floor. They were totally ignorant of cleanliness and other hygienic measures. The animal excretions and kitchen refuse were thrown before their own houses and would stink. The entire family slept in one room—men, women and children all huddled together, and often the domestic animals also found refuge in the same room. The thing they called bed was a bag stuffed with straw and raised from the ground upon which a pillow was placed. In the streets there were no gutters, pavements and no lighting. The largest town in Europe did not have more than twenty-five thousand inhabitants.

These were the conditions of Europe up to the eleventh century and even after, as admitted by the European historians themselves. Let us now look at the cities of Islamic Civilization, such as Baghdad, Damascus, Cordoba, Granada and Isabella.

Cordoba was the capital of Muslim Andalusia during the period of the Umayyid ruler, ʿAbd al-Raḥmān III. During the night it was illuminated with street lamps and one could walk for ten miles without any difficulty. All the streets were properly paved and all the waste was removed from the public roads. The entire city was surrounded by dense groves. Anybody coming to the city would enter it after a pleasant walk through these groves and public parks. The number of its inhabitants was more than a million. It had 900 public baths, 283,000 houses and 80,000 castles and palaces. There were 600 mosques. The outer circumference of the city was 30,000 yards. All the inhabitants were educated and in the eastern sector of the town alone 170 women worked as scribes of the Quran, writing the Quran in the Kūfi script. There were 80 schools where the poor students received educational instruction free of charge and there were also 50 hospitals. As for its mosques, to this day they are unique aspects of architectural beauty and novelty of design. The minaret was 70 feet high and its dome rested on props of fine wood. The entire mosque rested on 1093 pillars, built of various kinds of marbles which were in rows resembling a chessboard, 19 columns lengthwise and 38 breadthwise. More than 4,700 lamps illumined the mosque at night, consuming 24,000 pounds of olive oil annually. In its southern section, there were 19 doors made of an amazing kind of bronze plate. However, the central gate had plates of gold fixed to it. Similarly, there were 9 gates to the east and 9 gates to the west side of the mosque, each resembling the southern gates. As for the pulpit of the mosque, it would be sufficient to quote the English historians, "Whatever the human eye has witnessed, this is the most beautiful of them all, and its craftsmanship and splendour are not to be found in any of the ancient or modern monuments."

In close vicinity to Cordoba was a grand palace of al-Zahra. From the point of view of its architectural merits and splendour, it is regarded as one of the wonders of the world. The Turkish historian, Zia Pasha writes, "This palace is such a wonder of the world that a concept of the design of this type could not occur to any human being from the dawn of creation to this day. Human intellect has through the ages failed to produce a parallel in terms of the beauty of its design."

The dome of the palace rested on 4316 columns made of different kinds of marble with similar embellishments. Its floor was paved with marble slabs of various colors in beautiful designs, whilst its walls were panelled with sky blue and gold. Within the palace there were streams of clean fresh water, which passed through marble tanks that joined in an enormous and beautiful pond in the palace of the Caliph. A golden duck set with a pearl on its head could be seen at the centre of the pond. This huge pond had beautiful fish of all colors and varieties, which were fed on 12,000 loaves of bread every day.

There was a special parlor called "the Palace of Caliphate," whose ceiling and walls were built of various kinds of marble interspersed with gold. In the centre of this palace was a tank filled with mercury. On all four sides of this parlor were eight arched gates made out of ivory and ebony set with gold and pearls of all kinds and which rested on lofty columns made of colored stones and stainless marble. Sunlight entered through these gates and the rays illuminated the walls and the centre of the floor. The brilliance was enough to dazzle the inmates. The Caliph, al-Nāṣir, if he was in a frivolous mood, would just make a gesture to some servant who would set the mercury in the tank in motion to frighten any one gathered around him. This would convert the entire scene into one of lightning. The whole assembly was terror stricken by the allusion of the palace and all within it flying into the air. This allusion lasted until the mercury on the tank came to rest. The place was surrounded by thick groves on all sides and outside it were large open fields. Furthermore, this magnificent building was reinforced by 300 towers for military purposes. The al-Zahra Palace comprised the mansions of the Caliph, the nobles and female members of the family, and there were some halls in which the Caliph held court. The place where the Caliph took his seat was on a raised platform, over which there used to be a dome built with bricks of silver and gold. When Qāḍī Mundhar ibn Saʿīd severely criticised the Caliph in a large gathering in the congregation mosque of Cordoba, for the use of gold and silver in that manner, he had it demolished and rebuilt with ordinary bricks. Within the compound of this magnificent and vast palace there were also factories where various items, including clocks, medicine and book bindings, were made. There was a factory for decoration items and ornaments, sculpture, ship-building and image-forming. The construction of the al-Zahra Palace took four years. On a daily basis, 600 stones were hewn and fashioned into the required shape, not counting the stones used for paving the floor. More than 10,000 laborers worked and 1,400 mules were used, and every third day 1,100 camels laden with lime and other ingredients of mortar came to the site. As for the mosque of al-Zahra, 1,000 skilled men used to work, including 300 masons, 200 carpenters, 500 men of unskilled labor and some other craftsmen. It was completed within 48 days, and it is difficult to find a parallel of such speedy construction of an extraordinary building.

In 351 AH, al-Mustanṣir welcomed the King of Christian Spain, Ordon ibn Azfonish, in this magnificent palace. When he entered al-Zahra and witnessed its grandiosity, its splendour, its workers, its weaponry and its furnishings, he was dumbfounded. When he got to the assembly of al-Mustanṣir, he saw at his side heads and leaders of the State and noblemen included among whom were great scholars, orators and military generals. The Spanish King approached the Caliph al-Mustanṣir, took off his crown, put down his shroud and remained bear-headed until the Caliph allowed him to come near him. When face to face with the Caliph, he fell in prostration before him, stood up, walked a few steps and again prostrated. By the time he reached the Caliph, he had repeated this prostration, out of extreme awe, several times. He then kissed the Caliph's hand and retraced his steps with his face to the Caliph so that he may not be found guilty of turning his back to the Caliph. With this respectful attitude he occupied the seat prepared for him. The Caliph welcoming him said, "We welcome your arrival here. Let this visit of yours be a happy occasion for you, since we have a much better opinion of you and greater acceptance of you than you can ever expect." When these words were translated to him, he became pleased, bowed down at his place and kissed the ground and said, "I am a humble slave of my lord, Amīr al-Mu'minīn. On his grace I put my trust and look forward to be being favored by him. I have perfect faith in him and his men. So whatever service he entrusts me, and in whichever position he is gracious enough to keep me, I hope to proceed with sincere intent and purely from a point of view wishing well and doing good." At this, the Caliph said to him, "You hold a great position in our regard, and we hope our honoring you and holding you in esteem will be a source of pride for you among your own people, and that you will find what advantages you derive through inclining towards us as living under our protection."

The words pronounced by the Caliph al-Mustanṣir must have been pronounced with such force and grandeur, for on hearing them the Spanish King prostrated before him, prayed for his long life and prosperity, and assured him of his support.

In Granada, the greatness of architecture appears before us in the form of al-Hambra. It was such an amazing sight such that those looking at it would be taken aback. In spite of the ravages of the cruel hand of time, even today it is a centre of attraction for the tourists of the world. This palace was constructed on the foothill plain of the mountain of Granada in the vast expanse of lush green fields, which surrounded on all sides. Thus this building is regarded among the most beautiful buildings of the world. It had spacious halls and large rooms such as a black stone hall, two adjacent rooms built of white and black stones, a courtroom and a room to receive ambassadors. In a short discourse like this it is not possible for us to depict all the merits and beauties of al-Hambra. It suffices to mention what the French poet, Victor Hugo, says in his address to it, "O al-Hambra! O al-Hambra! O the palace which the angels decorated according to the wishes of imagination, and adjudged thee as a symbol of order and good taste, dexterity and skill. O thou castle of greatness and glory! In thee, decoration in the form of flowers and engravings of bent down branches are worth sight. When the silver rays of the moon, passing through thy western minarets, fall on thy walls, during the stillness of the night, a whisper is heard which fascinates those with hearts that feel."

The account of other cities of Andalusia and the description of their greatness and progress, is a long story. It would suffice to mention that in Isabella alone there were 6,000 looms to weave silken cloth. This city was surrounded on all sides by olive groves, and for this reason there were a hundred thousand olive pressers.

All the towns of Andalusia were densely populated, and every city was well known for some particular industry. Spanish helmets and armours were very popular. Steel was cast into various moulds for all purposes, particularly to make weapons. Orders from all over Europe were received. Zeno writes in his book, *Invasion of France*, "When the Arabs invaded the south of France from Andalusia and under the leadership of al-Samḥ al-Khulānī, Anbasah al-Kalbī and al-Ḥūr al-Thaqafī and conquered Arabonah, Fartashonah, Afnion and Lyon, they were armed with such weapons which were not to be found even in the British military."

Returning to the eastern wing of the Islamic world, there were many large cities with wonderful civilizations. Baghdad, before its expansion, was a small village, to which traders from the neighboring lands would gather at the end of every year. When the well-known ʿAbbāsid Caliph, Manṣūr decided to build and extend it, he brought together great engineers and architects. He also called in the agricultural experts to survey and allot the land. He laid the first brick of its building and said, "In the name of Allah, the Most Merciful, the Most Beneficent. All Praises are for Allah, which he who wants from among His servants, inherits it and Paradise for those who are conscious of Allah." He then said, "Proceed with the building with the blessing of Allah." The total expense for its construction was 4,800,000 dirhams. The number of workers reached 100,000. There were three walls of the city adjacent to one another. The eastern wing of the city had 6,000 roads and lanes, and in the western section, 4,000. Besides the rivers Tigris and Euphrates, there were offshoots of 11 major canals, whose water ran to every section of the town and every house in it. On the River Tigris alone, there were innumerable ferry points and 30,000 ferries to take people across the waters. There were 60,000 public baths in the city, although, during the last days of the ʿAbbāsid rule, this number had reduced to 10,000. The number of mosques had reached 300,000. As for the correct estimate of its population, due to the large number of scholars, men of letters and philosophers, it would be difficult to provide an estimate.

Abū Bakr al-Khaṭīb writes about Baghdad:

While mentioning Baghdad we missed some of its characteristics which Allah has made unique to Baghdad and which are not to be found anywhere else in the Eastern and the Western world. Among them were the courtesy of the citizens, good traits of their characters, palatable fresh water, an abundance of tasty fruits, general prosperity, expertise in every kind of industry, facilities for meeting every need and immunity from the propagation of [religious] innovations. In addition, there was an abundance of scholars, students, jurists, law-students, outstanding scholastics, mathematicians, grammarians, the best poets, the reporters of historical facts and genealogies, experts of arts and literature being drawn from far and near. In short, a presence of the fruit of everything, in a single period of time. If a citizen found his house inadequate for his needs it would be very easy for him to find a better residence. If somebody liked a house other than his own it would not be difficult to make such a transfer. The citizens could obtain their residences in any quarter of the town they came to have a liking for. If a person fleeing his enemies went to Baghdad, it would be very easy for him to seek asylum, for so many people would come forward and receive shelter and protection. He would be offered the facilities of every kind and could easily make any changes he deemed fit in his programme to meet the newly arising situations. The big traders, kings, the nobles and affluent persons living in lofty mansions were always ready to give charity and offer generous help to those in need and of a lower financial status. These were the bounties of Allah whose real nature and position are only known by Him.

The same author writes in another place:

Baghdad was a city that had no parallel on the face of the earth in its grandeur, glory, and greatness. There was a large number of

> scholars and nobles with no distinction between the elite, the learned people and the common folks. There was also an abundance of mosques, public baths, hotels and shops which were free from dust. There was clean palatable water, cool shades and the good weather of summer and winter. The health-giving effects of both the spring and autumn blessed the population. This city had reached its peak during the period of Hārūn al-Rashīd, and its population had also become great in number when it had the best shelters and the best resources of food. On every side there was verdure and freshness and the streets were crowded with pedestrians. However, a period of decline followed as people were in distress and the city became deserted, depopulated and desolate. Entire families abandoned the town en-block. There was chaos and people were miserable. However, there was a time when this city was distinguished from all other cities and stood unique among them in every way.

In the period of al-Muqtadir Billah and when the envoy of the Roman Emperor visited Baghdad, it had reached great splendour and glory. In Baghdad, the House of the Caliphate alone was greater than the greatest of the Syrian towns. When the envoy of the Roman Emperor visited Baghdad, he was accommodated at the Guest House. From the Guest House to the House of the Caliphate the army lined both sides of the road and numbered 160,000, both cavalry and infantry. He covered the distance between the Guest House and the House of the Caliphate between these two rows of armed men. When he greeted the Caliph it was ordered that he should be taken around the House of the Caliphate and shown everything. The residence of the Caliph had been vacated and no one was there except 7,000 attendants, 700 door keepers and 4,000 servants. Here, the treasures of the empire and the military arms were displayed. When this envoy was ushered into the House of the Tree, he was dumfounded at the sight of it. This tree was made out of silver, weighed 500,000 dirham and spread out into 18 large branches, branching off further into many smaller ones. On these branches rested various kinds of birds, some silver and others gold. The leaves of this tree were of different designs and colors and trembled as if moved by a gentle breeze. All these silver and golden birds were perched at such angles that air from natural directions entered their open beaks and the waves thus set into motion made music like that of the chirping and songs of the living birds in their natural state. Nearby, there were 15 statues of horsemen in silk brocade that held short lances in their hands. They had been shown chasing one another.

After that, the envoy entered the palace called al-Firdaws. The number of weapons in it could not be counted. He was then taken from one palace of the period of the Caliph Hārūn to another and visited twenty-three palaces in all. So tiring were these visits that he had to rest seven times before being finally led to the assembly hall in the presence of the Caliph al-Muqtadir Billah.

The historians mention that the number of carpets that were laid down in the House of the Caliphate for the envoy of the Roman Emperor was 22,000, excluding the carpets that were in the palaces. There were 38,000 silk and gold embroidered curtains hung in the various palaces on this occasion. The places visited by the envoy of the Roman Emperor also included the

Dār al-Wuḥūsh. In it, were different kinds of wild and domestic animals. There was an elephant house with four female elephants, and to look after each elephant there were eight Indian attendants. There was also a lion house which had 100 lions, 50 on either side of the building. An attendant held every lion and other beast of prey.

After visiting the House of the Caliphate, the envoy of the Roman Emperor was astounded, since there was no other palace on the face of the earth like the one he had just seen.

The evidence provided testifies to the greatness, strength, splendour and glory of the cities, palaces, mansions and other edifices of the Islamic Civilization.

ABOUT THE AUTHOR

Dr. Mustafa Sibaʿī was born in 1915 in Ḥums, Damascus. He memorized the Quran at an early age and completed his primary and secondary studies in the Masʿūdiyyah School. Constantly excelling in his studies, he became renowned for his intelligence and his academic brilliance. He studied the Islamic Sciences both with his father, Shaykh Ḥasanī Sibaʿī and in circles with the great scholars and jurists of Ḥums. His teachers included Shaykh Ṭāhir al-ʿAtāsī (Mufti of Ḥums at the time), Shaykh Zāhid al-ʿAtāsī, Shaykh Muḥammad al-Yāsīn, Shaykh Anas Kalālib and others.

From the age of eighteen he delivered the Friday *khuṭba*s in the absence of his father, and in 1933, he went to Egypt to enroll at the University of al-Azhar to study *Fiqh*. Upon completing his studies of *Fiqh*, he enrolled at the Uṣūl al-Dīn Faculty of al-Azhar where he excelled in his research. In 1949, he completed his Ph.D. on the theme of "The Position of Sunnah in Legislation."

He then embarked on a career in teaching and taught Arabic and Islamic Studies in the secondary schools of Ḥums. Later, he moved to Damascus where he established an educational institution which then set up branches throughout Syria.

In 1950, he was appointed as the Professor of Law at the Faculty of Laws, University of Damascus, and in 1955, he established the Faculty of *Sharīʿah* at the same university, becoming the first Dean of Faculty. Dr. Sibaʿī was elected to the Syrian Parliament to represent the people of Damascus from 1949-1954. Whilst in Egypt, he had met Imām Ḥasan al-Banna and joined the Muslim Brotherhood. There, he was imprisoned several times due to his *daʿwah* activities and his resistance to the British colonization of Egypt. Upon returning to Syria in 1945, he established the Muslim Brotherhood.

Dr. Sibaʿī founded several newspapers and magazines such as *al-Manār* and *Shahab*. In 1952, he was exiled to Lebanon where he set up a movement among the youth of Lebanon. In 1956, there was an assassination attempt made on his life, and it was later discovered that foreign powers had played a major part in the attempt.

Dr. Mustafa Sibaʿī attended many conferences and headed a delegation to the International Islamic Conference in Pakistan in 1951. On returning to Syria from Lebanon in 1956, he was sent on an academic tour of Western universities. He visited Turkey, Italy, Britain, Ireland, Belgium, Germany, Holland, Norway, Switzerland, Finland, Sweden and France where he met and discussed with Orientalists. In 1957, he was invited to Moscow by the University and consequently visited the majority of universities in Russia.

On Saturday July 3, 1964, he passed away, leaving behind a rich legacy of thought and action. Amongst his famous sayings, actually written from his hospital bed, the following is perhaps one of the most poignant, "I have seen people whose body is ill but whose heart is healthy. I have seen people whose body is healthy but whose heart is ill and very rarely have I seen the body and the heart both healthy."